ASPECTS OF BUDDHISM

ASPECTS OF BUDDHISM

by
HENRI de LUBAC, S.J.

Translated by
GEORGE LAMB

SHEED AND WARD
NEW YORK · 1954

Nihil Obstat: Carolus Davis, S.T.L.
Censor Deputatus
Imprimatur: E. Morrogh Bernard
Vic. Gen.
Westmonasterii, die 6a Julii, 1953

B L 1453
L 92
CO. 2

FOREWORD

THERE is no lack of good books in English for anyone who wishes to embark upon the study of Buddhism. It has nevertheless seemed advisable to preface the three specialised studies which make up this little volume with a brief sketch for the benefit of those readers who have not yet made acquaintance with the Law of Buddha. This sketch is, in a sense, of a purely material nature, whereas the studies that follow aim to elucidate the spirit of Buddhism.

(i) There seems to be no doubt that it was in the year 563 B.C. that there was born in Northern India, of the royal family of the Sakyas, the person who was to be known as Sakyamuni (the sage of the Sakya tribe), Bhagavat (the Blessed One), the Tathagata (he who "came in the same way", i.e. like the Buddhas before him), the Buddha (the Enlightened One, the Awakened One, the one who knows).

Legend shows him, after a youth spent in the lap of luxury, forsaking his father's palace, abandoning his wife and little son, and devoting himself to the "noble quest" in search of "deliverance". For seven years he sits at the feet of different masters of wisdom, devoting himself in turn to abstruse studies, fasts and the mortifications and disciplines whose aim is mystical ecstasy. But he discovers that not one of these ways leads to "disgust with the world, the absence of passion, the suppression of 'samsara' [the cycle of becoming, transmigration]—to nirvana". Rapt in his lonely meditation he arrives one day at the place known ever since as Buddha Gaya, and there, sitting under a fig-tree, he meditates. Suddenly, in the middle of the night, enlightenment comes: from then on he is the Buddha.

Having overcome Mara, the god of evil, and the more subtle temptation to keep his secret to himself, he then, on the entreaty of the great god Brahma Sahampati, begins his long career as a wandering preacher. His first sermon is delivered at the gates of Benares to an audience of five monks who had shown themselves well disposed towards him: "Come closer, O monks, live in holiness and put an end to misery!" From that day "there were six saints in the world". The Buddhist community had been founded. Accompanied by an increasing number of disciples, Sakyamuni travels all over North-East India. He converts King Bimbisara, Brahmans, young noblemen. After forty years, at the age of about eighty, he dies, or rather he "enters into pari-nirvana" (perfect nirvana). He had given his last instructions to his disciples, especially to his beloved Ananda: "Do not complain, do not despair, Ananda! From everything that man loves you must separate yourself. . . . In truth, O disciples, everything that becomes is perishable. Fight without ceasing!"

(ii) The essentials of the Buddhist teaching are contained in the Canon of the Sacred Scriptures. This appears in two main forms, the Pali Canon and the Sanskrit Canon (Chinese and Tibetan versions). In both it is made up of three parts (hence its name, the "Triple Basket": Tripitaka); the *Sutras*, an enormous collection of sermons and moral fables which the Buddha himself is supposed to have uttered; the *Vinaya* ("discipline"), a collection of monastic laws; the *Avhidharma*, a collection of moral and metaphysical treatises.

Of this great mass of material only a small proportion dates back to anywhere near the origin of the religion. There is nothing that in this respect resembles our New Testament; and so it is very difficult to re-create the earliest state of the doctrine, or to trace the early history of the religion, or even to know anything of a precise nature about the Buddha himself, although his historic existence and the main features of his moral personality are sufficiently well attested. This last point is, however, of little importance from the Buddhist point of view, for the empirical nature of the Buddha only plays a secondary part compared with the doctrine. "The Buddhas only point the way. . . . The Law which I have given you will be your master when I disappear."

(iii) When a person wishes to be converted to the Buddhist faith he repeats the formula of the "Triple Refuge": "I go to the Buddha, to the Dharma, to the Sangha for refuge."

The Sangha is the brotherhood. It is primarily an order of monks (bhikshus), around which gravitate, like a sort of third order, the laymen (Upasakas: devotees). Only the first have really entered upon the way that leads to deliverance. The others, who are still involved in the life of the world, content themselves with practising a certain natural morality, giving alms to the bhikshus, and practising the worship of Buddha. This worship is very simple, involving no sacrifice but only the veneration of images and relics of the Buddha and the sacred texts.

Entry is made into the Order in two stages: the Pravrajya or "departure", at the beginning of the novitiate; the Upasampaga or "arrival", a kind of profession which does not, however, necessitate any vows in the proper sense of the word. The monastic life does not involve any manual labour but religious offices, begging for food and spiritual exercises (both physiological and mental). The monastic ideal is an ideal of renunciation —of poverty and chastity; it is an ideal of the "middle way", of calm and inner freedom. Prostrate at the feet of Kassapa, the incarnation of this ideal, the gods ("devas") say:

Ancient One! Thou art emptied of desires:
The light in thy eyes is as pure as the lotus flower.

Naturally, during the course of twenty-five centuries and with the spread of the religion into many different lands, there have been enormous variations in its rules, in zeal and laxity.

(iv) The Dharma is the Law or Doctrine. It consists in brief in the four "holy truths", the subject of the sermon of Benares. These are concerned with misery; the origin of misery; the suppression of misery; the way which leads to the suppression of misery.

Everything in existence involves misery because everything is impermanent. Whether it is recognised or not, misery is intrinsic to every experience. Now this misery, like impermanence itself, has its origin in ignorance, which gives rise to desire, which in turn gives rise to becoming, and so on: this is samsara, the fatal wheel of becoming, both individual and universal. To put an end to it, it is necessary "to dry up desire", "to tear up the roots of desire", by destroying ignorance.

In other words, it means escaping from the law of karma, or action. It means preventing action from fructifying in becoming. It is true that a morally good action brings its reward, just as an evil action engenders punishment, because of an immanent force. But this reward itself is evil in so far as it exists within the world of becoming. "Evil is everything that aims at the happiness of this world." Only the absence of action, or "pure action", performed without any kind of attachment or desire, gains the "fruit of rupture": "Sinners go to the hells; those who have lived well go to the paradises; but those who have meditated on the right way, freed from the flow of action, will go to nirvana."

(v) The Marga (the Way). The "way which leads to the suppression of misery" is threefold.

First of all there is the Svarga-marga (the way to the paradises). This is the way taken by the Upasakas. It is the way of morality. But the paradises to which it leads are still part of our material world, the "world of desire" (kamadhatu). They are not deliverance. The gods who inhabit them, however great and however long their happiness, will be reborn into other conditions. In order to proceed towards deliverance it is therefore necessary to pass beyond this first way.

One "enters upon the true way" by taking the second

way, dhyanaloka-marga (the way to the heavens of recollection). This has eight stages, eight degrees of dhyana (recollection, ecstasy), by which one rises into the two vast regions of being which lie above our world—the "world of forms" (Rupadhatu) and the world "of the absence of forms" (Arupadhatu). One thus passes from the condition known as "trembling with joy" to "happiness without joy", then to "abstract felicity", followed by "expressionless quietude". Then come the other states of recollection known as "the infinity of space", "the infinity of knowledge", "the non-existence of everything", finally "neither with nor without thought".

Despite their verbal subtleties, these mystical stages are records of experiences, to achieve which Buddhism has to a certain extent at least borrowed the methods of the ancient Yogis.

(vi) At the eighth degree of dhyana, i.e. "neither with nor without thought", one reaches Bhavagra, "the summit of the world", the extreme point of existence. This is still not the end, however, for there still remains a subtle attachment, each detachment from a lower state having been obtained through the desire for the following state. If there is not to be a relapse and a return to the infernal round of becoming, detachment from Bhavagra is now necessary. With this one enters upon the third way, Nirvanamarga.

The way to nirvana is governed according to the particular spiritual temperament concerned, either by mystical intuition or by meditation on the doctrine; but in everyone intuition must be impregnated with wisdom, and wisdom, if it is to assist towards salvation, must be impregnated with mysticism: "No Prajna without Samadhi, no Samadhi without Prajna." Their union produces the spark of Enlightenment. This brings the full realisation of the condition in which one has "laid down the burden, cut the bonds", and can say with absolute certainty: "Existence is exhausted for me; I have lived through the spiritual life, there is nothing left to make me be reborn." This is the condition known as "nirvana upon earth" or "the nirvana with something remaining", as a prelude to the "nirvana with nothing remaining", or "perfect nirvana", at the end of this final existence.

(vii) What then is this perfect nirvana, the end of all Buddhist aspiration? Sakyamuni refused to disclose this. Some Buddhist schools, and a number of Westerners, have equated it with nothingness, and the numerous passages denying any kind of substantial personality, such as the metaphor of "the lamp that goes out", have provided them with grounds for argument. In reality, however, despite its negative vocabulary, Buddhism does seem to admit an "Immortal One" (amarita), an "Immovable One", an "Unshakable One", an ultimate state described as one of "confidence, calm, beatitude, delicacy, limpidity, freshness". "The idea of nirvana seems to be derived from experiences of ecstasy from which one awakens refreshed and comforted" (Colebrooke).

Nevertheless, Buddhism does not believe in any substantial principle of individuality, nor in any substantial Absolute above or at the heart of the universe. And its general direction (at least in the early stages) is pragmatist: it is not a case of seeking for union with the Principle of the Universe but of escaping from the misery of this world, finding the "way out", and obtaining "deliverance". Hence the perpetually negative vocabulary.

(viii) The Buddha did not want his disciples to concern themselves with purely speculative problems: "Just as, O monks, the open sea has only one savour, the savour of salt, thus, O monks, the doctrine of the Tathagata has only one savour, the savour of deliverance." Nevertheless the Buddhists soon split up into different schools. They also, at about the beginning of the Christian era, split up into two main branches, though there was no violent schism. These are known as the Hinayana (the Little Vehicle, a term of contempt) and the Mahayana (the Great Vehicle).

The Hinayana, as it has for long existed (especially in Ceylon, Burma and Siam), is not identical with primitive Buddhism; it is altogether more conservative, more sober, more specifically monastic. The Mahayana, which has developed chiefly in the Far East, has been richer in developments and more receptive to outside influences.

The Hinayana recognises a series of earthly Buddhas (predecessors of Sakyamuni and the future Buddha Maitreya); the Mahayana includes mystical or transcendent Buddhas as well, especially the five great Buddhas, each with its "double" (it has been called their "word"), or great Bodhisattva. The most famous duo is that of the Buddha Amitabha and his Bodhisattva Avalokitesvara (who becomes in China Kwan-yin and in Japan Kwannon): the worship of these is known as Amidism, which forms a kind of religion, apparently monotheistic in nature, within the vast world of Buddhism.

For the Hinayana the perfect type is the arhat, the monk who is holy "for himself", who knows that he will not be born again; for the Mahayana it is the bodhisattva, who, moved by a universal compassion, does not want to disappear into nirvana while there remains anyone on earth to be saved.

In the Mahayana the actual worship becomes more magnificent, the reason being that a greater part is played in it by the upasakas, and also that the Buddhas tend to appear as saviours. But the personality of Sakyamuni often becomes blurred by the figures of other Buddhas.

(ix) The "Triple Basket" of the Mahayanist Canon "has no lid", which means to say that numerous works have been added to the Canon. They contain revelations supposed to have been made by the Buddha to celestial bodhisattvas and said to contain the fundamental doctrine. The most important are the *Prajnaparamita* ("The Perfection of Wisdom"), the *Lalitavistara* ("The Unfolding of the Games", a miraculous account of the Buddha's life), the *Lankavatara* (the Law given to the island of Lanka, i.e. Ceylon), the *Saddharmapundarika* ("The Lotus of the Good Law"). These books give the "absolute truth", whereas the books of the Hinayana only give a "relative truth".

Two main schools of metaphysical idealism have developed in the Mahayana: the Madhyamika (founded by Nagarjuna) and the Yogacara (found by Asanga). Whereas the Hinayana insisted on the purely relative character of the phenomena of which the universe is composed, these Mahayanist schools insist on universal emptiness. For anyone who has properly understood it, there is no real distinction between one thing and another anywhere: "Nirvana is. samsara and samsara is nirvana." This is the doctrine of the "nirvana which is not an absolute end." Any distinction between one thing and another is only apparent and the individual Buddha has never existed (Docetism). The Yogacara school develops an idealism of a less purely negative kind with its doctrine of the "Nothing but thought" and its grandiose construction of the Trikaya or "the Three Bodies of the Buddha".

(x) Despite its origins, Buddhism is universalist in character. Sakyamuni did not preach to any one single caste or people but to everybody. He wanted the Dharma to be preached to each person in his own language. Buddhism has spread throughout all the countries of Asia, not as a fact of culture helping to make the wheels go round, but rather as a faith carried by missionaries. The "gift of religion" it holds to be the greatest gift of all. Wherever it has spread Buddhism has adapted itself to its environment with a generous flexibility.

CONTENTS

CHAPTER I

BUDDHIST CHARITY

The person with a hundred different loves
Has a hundred different pains.
The person with ninety different loves
Has ninety different pains.
The person with eighty different loves . . . etc.
The person with one love
Has one pain.
The person without love
Has no pain. [1]

THIS quotation, which with its negative tone of disillusionment sounds so typically Buddhist, seems to justify the opinion of those historians for whom there can be no possible question of charity in Buddhism. The position is not quite so simple, however; a closer examination of it may enable us to modify— in one direction or the other—some fairly common interpretations of Buddhism, and at the same time to enter a little more deeply into its spirit.

One of the first obligations laid upon every Buddhist is that of ahimsa, i.e. "not-harming". This rule existed before Buddha, is very important in Jainism and still exists in modern Hinduism. Ahimsa means primarily—it is thus that it is almost always envisaged—respect for all living things. [2] But in the teaching of Śakyamuni, at least, it has a wider significance. "Any act which is harmful to others is a sin." Consequently, "When you wish to perform an action, consider whether it is going to be harmful to others, harmful to yourself, harmful to yourself and others: if it is, do not perform it; for it is an evil action whose fruit will be suffering"; whilst the *Jatakamala* has a more succinct saying, which exactly recalls the words of Jesus: "Do not do unto others that which you would not wish them to do unto you."[3]

But ahimsa is no more than a beginning. Despite what Lehmann[4] has said, it by no means embodies the whole of the Buddhist's duty to his neighbour. This includes a number of other obligations, at once positive and negative,[5] which can be reduced to the three essential virtues signified by the three names maitri, dana and karuna. It is only after studying all three of these that we can know in what sense it is permissible to speak of Buddhist charity, what place this holds in the general economy of Buddhism, and how it is to be regarded in relation to Christian charity.

The best English word for maitri (metta)[6] seems to be "loving-kindness". It means a certain feeling, a certain state of mind, which is unassuming and gentle, but warm and friendly, and which should be habitually maintained. It is superior to any kind of practical activity; from it alone, in fact, does the latter derive any value it may possess. This is made clear in the *Itivuttaka* in the following splendid passage:

> None of the means employed to acquire religious merit, O monks, has a sixteenth part of the value of loving-kindness. Loving-kindness, which is freedom of heart, absorbs them all; it glows, it shines, it blazes forth.
>
> And in the same way, O monks, as the light of all the stars has not a sixteenth part of the value of the moonlight, but the moonlight absorbs it and glows and shines and blazes forth: in the same way, O monks, none of the means employed to acquire religious merit has a sixteenth part of the value of loving-kindness. Loving-kindness, which is freedom of heart, absorbs them; it glows, it shines, it blazes forth.
>
> And in the same way, O monks, as at the end of the rainy season, the sun, rising into the clear and cloudless sky, banishes all the dark spaces and glows and shines and blazes

forth: and in the same way again, as at night's end the
morning star glows and shines and blazes forth: so, O monks,
none of the means employed to acquire religious merit has a
sixteenth part of the value of loving-kindness. Loving-kindness, which is freedom of heart, absorbs them: it glows, it
shines, it blazes forth. [7]

Buddhist legend attempts to inspire this feeling of loving-
kindness when it says that "at the moment of the Buddha's
conception, all beings had loving and helpful thoughts towards
each other, all had the feelings of a father or a mother", and
when it describes Kassapa delivering this funeral oration over
his departed Master: "He was compassionate; no living thing
was ever hurt by him, for he was armed with mercy", [8] and
again when it shows the Buddha reproving the Brahmans for
having forgotten, amongst all the other ways of doing good,
the most important way, that of kindness. [9] And in point of
fact the teaching embodied in these legends was highly fruitful;
as a result, "Buddhism was able to inspire the peoples of the
Far East with an ideal of peaceful living and humanity". [10]

As nothing is more precious, so nothing is more powerful
than maitri. It alone can triumph over hatred: "Hatred has
never put an end to hatred. Loving-kindness puts an end to
hatred. This is the eternal law." [11] It triumphs over all wickedness: "Wickedness is like fire, and loving-kindness like water.
When water is used to put out fire there is no chance of it
failing." [12] In the person who has submitted to it with all his
heart, maitri has power to remove the gravest faults. A certain
Maitrakanyaka was fruitful in good works, he had given as
many as thirty-two pieces of gold to the monks; but one un-
lucky day he hit his mother because she objected to his going
overseas on business. Maitrakanyaka was shipwrecked and
landed on an island, where for some time he was entertained in
splendid houses by thirty-two beauties of paradise, the daughters
of his alms. But finally he arrived at a place of horror where
dwelt a man whose head was being eaten into by a red iron

disc. "What have you done to deserve this, unfortunate one?" he asked. "I committed a crime," the other replied, "and I must remain here until a criminal as wicked as myself arrives; but I cannot believe that any other man has ever done what I did—beaten his mother." Then Maitrakanyaka remembered his misdeed and immediately the gory disc fastened itself onto his head. But the pain inspired him to utter this sublime prayer: "May no one ever be unfortunate enough to come and take my place here!" And at once he was released from pain. [13]

As can be seen from this story, maitri may call for heroism. So Buddha understands it in his exhortations to his disciples:

> O monks, that man would not be fulfilling my commands who, even whilst ruffians were cutting him limb from limb with a saw, allowed hatred to fill his heart. Even then he should bestir himself and say: "This will not change my heart. I shall not utter evil words. I shall remain kindly and compassionate, with my heart full of loving-kindness and with no hatred within me, thus shedding light upon this man from my heart full of loving-kindness and free from hatred and malice." [14]

The Buddha himself had given an example of this sort of behaviour in his relationship with his wicked cousin Devadatta. This cousin, after using magic against Buddha and turning a number of his disciples away from him, had fallen ill; but from the "Peak of the Vulture", where he was then living, Sakyamuni stretched out his arm, touched his cousin's head and cured him. Again Devadatta attacked him; he took hold of a powerful catapult, fired it and wounded the Buddha. Blood began to pour from the wound, and nothing that the doctor Jivaka could do was of any avail. Then Kassapa exclaimed: "O Blessed One, if it is true that you harbour in your heart the same feelings for both your friends and your enemies, may the flow of blood cease!" And immediately the blood stopped gushing forth. [15]

No effort should be spared, then, to reach a state of mind at once so precious, so powerful, and, in certain cases, so difficult to attain. And so one of the chief exercises which the bhikshu has to perform consists in "meditating to acquire maitri". He proceeds by stages which are carefully graded. He must pray that all beings may obtain absolute felicity, but as he is not at first able "thus to direct his thoughts" he begins by dividing all beings into three categories—friends, acquaintances, enemies. The first and third categories he then subdivides into three groups—large, medium and small—making seven groups in all. The monk then prays for the happiness of his greatest friends. This he finds easy. He repeats his prayer, endeavouring to preserve the same intensity, for each group in turn, until he comes to his worst enemies. "When this impartial sevenfold meditation has been mastered he enlarges the area of his prayer, including in it towns and countries to the north, south, east and west, until finally he includes all living things in this one thought of loving-kindness."[16] This exercise can then be repeated in different forms, so that gradually he accustoms himself to living in the most meritorious condition of all:

One who, in the morning, at midday and in the evening, brings forth simply one spark of loving-kindness in his heart, gains more merit than one who, in the morning, at midday and in the evening, gives gifts of a hundred bowls of food. That is why, O monks, you must learn to say this: We want to bring forth loving-kindness, which frees the heart— bring it forth, increase it, develop it, appropriate it, exercise it, obtain it, and use it properly.[17]

These examples are enough to show that maitri is not, like ahimsa, entirely negative. It is not simply a case of suppressing hatred like any other passion or desire; not simply a case of not doing or wishing evil to anyone.[18] We shall see later what there is of truth behind this error. What seems to favour it, at first sight, is the negative vocabulary which has always been so dear to Buddhism, and its habit of expressing man's principal moral duties in a negative way. The five great commandments will be remembered: not to kill, not to steal, not to lie, not to give way to debauchery, not to get drunk. In Buddhism perhaps more than in any other religion sin has been compared to a defilement, and virtue conceived of as a quality—purity— which in itself seems merely negative.[19] Buddhist scholars are not afraid to define morality (sila) as "the cessation and non-repetition of sin".[20] Nevertheless, this explanation is not quite satisfactory, as even a critic as severe as Fr. Allo recognises: "The loving-kindness preached by Buddhism is, despite what is so often said, strictly positive."[21]

It is all the more so as it does not find its fulfilment merely in any inward feeling, but has to be translated into action. Maitri is not genuine if it does not lead to dana (giving). This is already made clear in the Little Vehicle. "The good man seeks his own good and that of others." And all the charitable actions which legend attributes to the Buddha, either during his final existence on earth or, more particularly, during his earlier lives, both human and animal, help to build up his disciple's ideal. One can choose examples at will from the rich storehouse of the Jatakas—usually simply Buddhist versions of stories dating from a much earlier period.

"India," writes de la Vallée-Poussin, "imagined the saint as a kind of penitent-scholar-mystic; but it had also conceived of a gentler and more humane kind of sanctity, whose heroes naturally tended to be animals. It told the story of the stag that laid its head on the sacrificial stone to save one of its hinds, of the monkey that made its body into a bridge, of the elephant that tore out its tusk to give it to the avaricious huntsman, of the good bear and the ungrateful man. To these noble animals it added a number of princes: Vessantara, who gave away his wife and children; Sibi, who saved a dove by feeding a vulture with his own flesh. All these moving tales of heroism crystallised round the figure of Sakyamuni. It was he who was believed to have been the hare, the monkey, the bear and the Sibi of the old legends."[22] Here we need only quote two of these stories: the one about the good stag, and the one about the king who gave his flesh to save a dove. Each was formerly commemorated by a stupa, erected near others on which were inscribed the most important events in the life of Sakyamuni.

A fire broke out one day on a barren plain situated in the heart of a vast forest. "The birds and beasts were reduced to a state of great distress. In front of them was a rapidly flowing river which brought them all to a halt. Maddened by the raging fire, they began throwing themselves into the water to their death. The stag, moved by pity, advanced into the torrent, and though it tore open his skin and shattered his bones, he did all he could to save them from drowning. The last to arrive was a lame hare, and the stag, triumphing over exhaustion and pain, had just enough energy to get it to the other side. But his strength had gone; he collapsed in the water and died. The gods collected his bones and erected a stupa to him."

A no less moving sacrifice was performed by the king of the Sibis—who was also, one day, after a series of reincarnations, to become the Buddha Sakyamuni.[23] This is one of the scenes most frequently portrayed in Buddhist art.[24] The god Indra had decided to test the king. "He took the form of a hawk pursuing a dove, or rather another god disguised as a dove, 'a dove with plumage as blue as the firmament and eyes like red pearls'. To escape from the hawk, the dove took refuge in the bosom of the king, but the hawk, asserting its own right to live, demanded its prey or an equal amount of living flesh in exchange. The king, with an act of great sacrifice, cut the flesh from his own legs. But, miraculously, the scale in which the dove had been placed continued to weigh heavier than the flesh which was to purchase its ransom; so that in the end the king had to put his whole body in the scale to save the bird.

Then Indra revealed his identity"—and proclaimed the future reincarnation.[25]

This ideal, which was kept constantly in the minds of the faithful by memories and legends about the Buddha, reached its full flowering in the Mahayana, in which loving-kindness takes on an increasingly active significance, manifested in the care of the sick,[26] by charitable institutions and by a fully developed missionary apostolate. The practice of medicine, which the monks were forbidden by the Little Vehicle, is allowed by the Great Vehicle as a means of serving one's neighbour. In certain districts, Buddhist monasteries have engaged in works of charity—though their activity in this domain is not to be compared with that of Christian monasteries[27]—and at the present day a considerable number of them are making great efforts to organise social work. Asoka, not satisfied with "gentleness towards all creatures", had "wells dug and medicinal herbs planted for men and animals"; he made "distributions to Brahmans and Shamans" and "the aged"; he freed prisoners; and he instituted "Officers of the Law" to watch over the administration of his alms.[28] The "Memoirs" of Huian Tsang explain in detail the kind of charity to which the Buddhist faith inspired the Emperor Harsha, the last Emperor of independent India in the seventh century of the Christian era (A.D. 606–647). "His rule," says Huian Tsang, "was one of justice and humanity . . . he forgot to eat and drink in his zeal to perform good works . . . in the towns, in the villages, at the meetings of the roads and at cross-roads, he had relief-huts built where food, drink and medical supplies were stored, to be given free to travellers and the poor.[29] "The Lotus of the Good Law" mentions similar kinds of activity. When in Chapter XVI it refers to those "who give to the religious brotherhoods household goods and medical supplies for the sick", it is simply restating one of the means employed from the very beginning by the upasakas in succouring the bhikshus. But in the first chapter the perspective is a wider one:

I see in many lands all the Bodhisattvas, equal in number to the sands of the Ganges.

Some are distributing alms—gold and silver and precious stones and coral; slaves, both male and female; horses, sheep . . . with joy in their hearts they are offering four-horse carriages decorated with balconies, flags, flowers and banners. Others are giving their sons, their wives, their daughters; others, their own flesh, which they love so dearly; others, their hands and feet . . . some are giving their head or eyes or their whole body—a thing so dear to man! And having distributed these alms, they then ask, calm in mind, for the knowledge of the Tathagata. . . . Some there are who distribute alms in the presence of the Jina, in the midst of the Assembly; they give great quantities of food, drink, rice, remedies. . . .[30]

Danaparamita—i.e. the perfection which consists in giving, generosity—is thus defined in the *Lieou tou tsi king*, a collection of sutras about the six Paramitas, translated into Chinese by Seng-houei:

It means this: helping men and animals with acts of loving-kindness; having compassion on the multitude who are in error; rejoicing that the wise have achieved salvation; protecting and helping all living beings; transcending the boundaries of heaven and earth with a charity as wide as a river and as large as the sea; performing acts of generosity to all living beings; feeding the hungry; giving drink to the thirsty; clothing those who are cold; refreshing those overcome by the heat; being ready to help the sick; whether it be carriages, horses, boats, equipment, or any kind of precious material or famous jewel, or beloved or son or kingdom—whatever it may be that you are asked to give, it means giving it at once.[31]

There is, moreover, a hierarchy of giving. Bodily assistance is not enough if it is not accompanied by an effort to assist the mind. Beginning at the lowest level with gifts of material goods,[32] charitable activity should aim at the ultimate deliverance of all beings. This is clearly taught in the *Samdhinirmocanasutra*, or "the Sutra which unties knots"—i.e. explains mysteries:

What is a bad means (anupaya)? When by the practice of the perfections the Bodhisattvas help others, but are content to supply them with merely material aid, without raising them from their misery or introducing them into beatitude, then they are using a bad means.

Why? Because material help is not sufficient. Whether a dunghill be large or small, it cannot possibly be made to smell sweet by any means whatsoever. In the same way, living beings are unhappy because of their acts, because of their nature; it is impossible to make them happy by supplying them with merely material aids. The best way of helping them is to establish them in goodness.[33]

Dana is not therefore a superficial altruism. If it must always follow from maitri it must also be inspired more particularly by karuna (compassion, pity). Little remains to be said about this; it has already appeared several times in the passages which we have quoted. It is at the root of the whole Buddhist law, which derives from an intuition of universal suffering. In the funeral oration, which according to the *Story of the Compilation of the Tripitaka* Kassapa delivered on Sakyamuni soon after his death, we read: "He was compassionate; no living being was ever hurt by him, for he was armed with mercy."[34] According to the canonical tradition Sakyamuni himself, once he had taken the decision to preach the Law which he had discovered, said:

The Buddha who has attained to peace
Is not a good man
If he does not endeavour to bring the world over
to the other bank.[35]

And the *Asokavadana*, in its account of the pilgrimage under-
taken by the pious Emperor Asoka to Buddha Gaya, makes his
companion, the venerable Upagupta, say: "It was here that
the Blessed One put to flight the daughters of Mara, by taking
compassion as his ally."[36] Again, the main part of the Sermon
of Benares ends with these words: "Come, monks, the Dharma
has been proclaimed. Be holy and put an end to suffering"; or:
"You have been freed: set out on your way therefore . . .
having compassion on all the world."[37] And the *Jatakamala*,
summarising the moral of all its stories, says: "The Law
prescribes many different actions and carries a whole series of
prohibitions, but it can be summed up in one phrase—pity for
all creatures." The same thought is to be found in a number
of other passages, of which we need quote only one, from the
Prajnakaramata. The great Bodhisattva Avalokiteshvara is
addressing the Buddha. "Lord," he says to him, "there is no
need to teach the Bodhisattvas a great number of rules. There
is one which includes them all. When a Bodhisattva is full of
Compassion he fulfils all the conditions required for Buddhahood—just as all the senses function in the person in whom life
is active."[38]

No more than maitri is karuna (which specifies it) a purely
negative state of mind. Nevertheless, it would be a mistake to
imagine it as a sentimental attachment or a violent emotion.
The man who knows may feel pity for those who do not know,
but the more purified his pity becomes, the less he is moved
by their sufferings; for, as we shall see later, the ultimate gain
is an absolute indifference. It is a power which remains
serene.[39] However this may be, its place is so fundamental to
Buddhism that it has been said that Buddhism "discovered
the moral value of man through compassion and suffering".[40]

These three independent virtues—maitri, dana and karuna—
were not absolutely new to India. As in a great many other
cases, the Buddha Sakyamuni was simply repeating here, in a
more popular and comprehensible form, teachings already
at least partly contained in the oldest Upanishads. In its fifth

lesson the *Brhad-Aranyaka-Upanishad* describes "devas, men and asuras" undergoing their novitiate under the direction of their father Prajapati:

When they had ended their novitiate the devas said: "Speak, lord!" Then he uttered the syllable *da* and added, "Do you understand?" "We understand," they replied. "You mean 'Overcome your passions (Damyata)'." "That is so," he replied, "you understand."

Then the men said to him: "Speak, lord!" And he uttered the same syllable, *da*, adding, "Do you understand?" "We understand," they replied. "You mean, 'Give! (Datta)'." "That is so," he replied, "you understand."

Then the asuras said to him: "Speak, lord!" To them too he uttered the same syllable, *da*, adding, "Do you understand?" "We understand," they replied. "You mean, 'Be compassionate (Dayadhvam)'." "That is so," he replied, "you understand."

This is what the voice of God says again and again when it speaks in the thunder: *da, da, da*—that is to say, overcome your passions, give, be compassionate. These are the three rules which must be taught: self-mastery, almsgiving, pity. [41]

It is not surprising, therefore, that these virtues are already to be found in the Little Vehicle. The Arhat does not simply aim at self-mastery. No doubt his ideal can be described as, on the whole, egoistic or individualistic—though it seems paradoxical to use such words to describe a doctrine whose aim is "de-individualisation"—but altruism is by no means absent from it. If each bhikshu pursues his own self-interest, and in his immediate actions is concerned principally with himself, the Sangha as a whole aims to diminish the number of miseries in the world. The teaching of the First Sermon was never forgotten completely [42]—the teaching of the first person "to seek mental concentration and absolute wisdom with the aim of saving all beings". [43]

Nevertheless, this charitable aspect was to be developed and deepened, above all, in the Great Vehicle, in which concern for the salvation of others is so predominant that Milarepa, the famous poet and mystic of Tibet, could write in his "Spiritual Testament":

The person who only thinks of his own salvation harvests samsara.
The person who does not distribute what he has gathered Meditates in vain; he will remain without virtue.[44]

In these words the joy of giving is exalted; the words "loving-kindness" and "pity" are no longer sufficient. Like Asanga, the great scholar of the Yogacara, we can here only speak of compassionate tenderness. This ideal of the Great Vehicle found wonderful artistic expression in the Indian paintings of the great Bodhisattvas,[45] often called "the Compassionate Ones".[46] According to this ideal, there is something better than holiness—the sanctification of others; something to be preferred to entry into nirvana—leading others towards it. Even before Vasubandhu, under the influence of his brother Asanga, went over to the Mahayana, he was proclaiming this ideal on the basis of the canonical texts.[47] Asanga and Santideva sing pure hymns in praise of it. Here we reach the highest peak of Buddhism—one of the highest peaks to which humanity has attained.

The Bodhisattva [says Asanga], has the love of creatures in his very bones, as one loves an only son. As a dove cherishes its little ones and will not move until it has hatched them out, so the Compassionate One loves the creatures, his children. . . .
The world is not able to bear its own misery. How much less then can it endure the misery of the mass of others! The Bodhisattva is the opposite of this; he is able to bear the misery of the whole mass of living creatures, of all who are

in the world. His tenderness towards creatures is the highest miracle in the universe; or rather no miracle at all, since he is identical with others, and creatures are like himself to him. . . .

At every moment, and for every creature, the Bodhisattva would like to create as many worlds as there are sands in the Ganges, each filled with the seven jewels. For his longing to give is insatiable, and he finds more happiness in giving than the others do in receiving. He looks upon the creatures whom he serves as more beneficent than himself, saying that they are the creation of the All-Perfect and Unsurpassable Illumination.[48]

Santideva is no less elevated and no less lyrical:

If the suffering of many is brought to an end by the suffering of one, the one should foster this suffering in himself by means of compassion. . . . The Bodhisattvas, finding their joy in smoothing away the sorrows of others, descend into hell as swans swoop into a clump of lotus flowers. The deliverance of creatures is for them an ocean of joy drowning everything else: what is the value of a half-hearted deliverance? . . . Have one passion only: the good of others. . . . All who are unhappy, are unhappy from having sought their own happiness. All who are happy, are happy from having sought the happiness of others. . . . You must exchange your well-being for the miseries of others.[49]

Such altruism has to be made effective *in opera et veritate*: "It is through actions that I shall proclaim the Law. What is the use of simply repeating the words? What good would an invalid get merely from reading a book on medicine?"[50] It is aware of its conditions, the most fundamental being the subjugation of pride: "There is someone doing a humiliating job; why should he, when I am there? If it is pride which prevents me from taking his place, may my pride perish!"[51] It is also aware of its two essential characteristics, universality and disinterestedness. The first of these is mentioned again and again in the passages we have quoted,[52] and it is fully recognised in every other branch of Buddhism too. Even in the *Sutta-Nipata*, for instance, it was written: "Cultivate an unlimited loving-kindness towards the whole world—to those above, below and on all sides of you; free from hatred, enmity and rivalry."[53] As for disinterestedness, this is clearly indicated in the definition which Santideva gives of maitri: "A desire, a need, a hunger for the happiness of others, a love [sueka] which remains untainted by either personal pleasure or the hope of return."[54] How this would have delighted Spinoza or his disciple Léon Brunschvicg![55] Finally, this altruism is equally clear as to the method which will enable it to take the place of egoism. Just as the bhikshu, as we have seen, practised loving-kindness in his solitary meditations, so the person who has entered on the "path to Buddha-hood" aims to develop a more radical state of mind by means of two mental processes: the identification of himself with others, and the substitution of his own ego for that of others. This is explained, again by Santideva, in Chapter VIII of the *Bodhicaryavatara*:

First, reflect deeply on the likeness which exists between yourself and others. "Since all have the same pains and the same joys as I have, I should care for them as I care for myself." The body, despite the differences between its various members, is looked after as a single thing: it should be the same with the world, in which different beings have their joys and sorrows in common. . . .

Reflecting on the fact that you are yourself full of faults and that others are brimming over with good qualities, you will endeavour to throw off your own personality and adopt that of others.

You are interested in your various members as parts of your own body: why not in men as parts of humanity?

The person who wants to save himself must practise the great secret: put himself in the place of others.[56]

Then: "O wonder! however impassive they may be in the face of even the greatest of their own sufferings, the Bodhisattvas, full of compassion, are moved by the miseries of others, however small these may be."[57]

Faced with the evidence of these passages, which in some cases sound so like our own, is it then possible to speak of Budhist charity, exactly as one speaks of Christian charity? Do Buddhist charity and Christian charity exist on the same level?

"Charity" was in fact the word chosen to translate "maitri" by Burnouf, the scholar who did so much to introduce the study of Buddhism into the West.

He thus justified his use of the word: "I have no hesitation in using 'charity' to translate maitri, for this means, not friendship, or the particular feeling of affection which a man may have for one or for several of his fellows, but a universal feeling which fills him with loving-kindness towards men and in general makes him always ready to help them. This . . . one of the characteristic features of Buddhist morality, is the virtue which seems to me to be signified by the word maitri. . . ."[58] The Buddhist moralist Edmond Laboulaye echoes Burnouf. "All the virtues," he says, "have their source in maitri, and this word can only be translated as 'charity' or 'love'."[59] Alfred de Vigny, meditating on the Buddha in 1862, wrote in his diary: "Charity is the essence of his religion." Much more recently Fr. Léon Wieger expressed the same opinion.[60] Taine,[61] Renan and many others maintained that Buddhism, like Christianity, is a "religion of charity". Amiel also uses the word in his Journal.[62] In the opinion of Renouvier, "the sovereign rule of Buddhism" is "a law of absolute love, absolute charity . . . exactly like the law of the Gospel"[63]—and this, coming from Renouvier, does not by any means signify unqualified approval. In both, he says, the lessons of love "have their source in the same feeling".[64] For Léon de Rosny "Buddhism, like Christianity, is essentially a law of love".[65] The German, Pischel, tried to prove this in detail; it was he who first drew attention to the beautiful passage in the *Itivuttaka* quoted above. At the end of his enquiry he found the "cardinal virtue" of Buddhism identical with the "cardinal virtue" of Christianity.[66] More recently, Henri Brocher could discover only a single point of difference between the two, a difference which had often been noted before: in the Christian religion, he wrote, charity remains "within the limits of reason and is restricted to man", whilst in Buddhism it is "extended to all the beings in creation and is absolutely unlimited".[67]

This opinion is not shared by everybody, however. We have only to remember those who, like Lehmann, can see only the negative side of the Buddhist rules and reduce them all, in practice, to ahimsa. Others, like Oldenberg—who was followed for a time by Foucher—maintain that Buddhist charity is "essentially egoistic and entirely occupied with personal salvation", that it "ends in itself and bears no resemblance at all to the overflowing altruism imagined by Taine".[68] This judgment, it is true, is due to their having based their entire study of Buddhism on Hinayanist books. But such is Keith's conclusion too. And however it may appear at first sight, we believe it to be nearer the truth than the view held by Burnouf and his followers. It was inevitable that, in the decades immediately following the scientific discovery of Buddhism in the last century, people should have been particularly sensitive to the analogies—which seemed at first sight so obvious—between the two great religions of the East and West. Even the upholders of Christianity were sometimes inclined to see illusory similarities between the two. But a fuller investigation of the sources, and a more patient analysis of the facts, were to bring out increasingly the essential characteristics of each—and hence their differences. In point of fact, the identification of Buddhism and Christianity made by Renouvier and more recent authors frequently arises from a misunderstanding of the exact nature of Christian charity.[69] Whatever may be the truth about the use of the word "charity" as a translation of maitri or any other Buddhist word, in my opinion the identification of Buddhist charity with Christian charity even when made with certain reservations, can only take place through misunderstanding, or, at least, a serious lack of analysis. Buddhism, even in its highest and most admirable forms, is entirely different in inspiration from Christianity. It corresponds to a different idea. It has a different place, in a different scheme of salvation. By making a comparison, only slightly exaggerated, between the two, we may manage to bring out into the full light of day the utterly different spirit informing the two religions.

Before we proceed to our final considerations, however, three preliminary observations seem to be called for.

In the first place, though there is every reason to believe that Sakyamuni himself—in so far as he can be discerned behind the mass of legend that grew up about him so long after his death—was a gentle, compassionate soul, full of loving-kindness and good works, it nevertheless remains true that the ideal of charity which developed in Buddhism grew out of beliefs which had absolutely no historical foundation at all. The Buddha, as he began to be depicted in his earlier existences, and the Bodhisattvas, are purely legendary creatures. All the books in which the miraculous stories about them occur—Pali and Sanskrit, Hinayanist and Mahayanist—are equally fictitious. "It would be astonishing," says Paul Oltramare, "to find that it had never occurred to Buddhist writers to draw their examples from the actual life of the day, if it was not clear that their chief interest lay far more in the glorification of their great saints than in any description of morality in action."[70]

Now—and this is the second point—this legendary character makes the ideal itself somewhat unreal and fantastic. The deeds which are related are often ridiculously far-fetched. Most of the stories are childish; taken as a whole, they contain more pathos than instruction.[71] India has been described as "more Greek than the Greeks" and Buddhist legend certainly justifies this description, for it is always tending to relapse into the monotonous, rather ridiculous hyperbole that seems to come so naturally to the trained mind and which so often makes it boring and tasteless.[72] It is capable of a kind of humanism that can be very delicate, but the Indian imagination has been allowed to spread itself far too freely in it. And it is entirely a case of imagination—the imagination which seeks to "improve upon nature"; but the world which it creates is no more than a dream-world. "One cannot help smiling at the Buddha's efforts to convert serpents, birds, vampires, harpies and all the other fantastic creatures" imagined by India.[73] His way of becoming all things to all creatures may be admirable as a charming piece of invention, but it is not very moving. For example, "when he was crossing a burning desert, millions of devas and spirits came rushing up to him to spread umbrellas over his head. He thereupon multiplied himself into as many little Buddhas as there were umbrellas, so that each spirit should have the satisfaction of believing that its pious offer had been accepted. One day he was faced by an impassable river. The good spirits immediately built him a number of bridges across it. The Blessed One multiplied himself according to the number of bridges, and each spirit imagined that he had passed over its own and nobody else's".[74]

No less childish and lacking in human depth—though it contains more pathos—is the legend of Visvantara, the young prince who had a passion for charity. This famous legend was transferred to the theatre and became the most popular of the Tibetan "mysteries".[75] Visvantara "owned a white elephant, which had the magic gift of being able to cause rain. A neighbouring king, whose country was suffering from drought, asked to be given the animal, and this Visvantara did. The citizens were furious and demanded that he should be punished, and for his excess of charity the young prince was obliged to go into exile, accompanied by his wife Madri, who was determined to share his fate, and their two children. As they went on their way two Brahmans asked him for his carriage-horses, so he gave them to them; then a third came along and asked for the carriage itself, and he gave this away too. Finally after endless sufferings, the poor family arrived at the forest in which they had decided to make their home: they were to live in a hut, feeding on roots and wild fruit. The trees, moved by compassion, inclined their branches of their own accord and offered their fruit to the two little boys. But another Brahman came along and asked the father to give him the two children as servants. Although the children were both terrified, and he himself heartbroken, the prince gave them to him. Finally the god Indra came along disguised as an ascetic and asked for the wife as a slave, and Visvantara gave her away too".[76] In the end, of course, Indra reveals his identity and the martyr to charity recovers his family and his goods. As will be realised, this can be very moving, both on the stage and as a story. But, says Oltramare, "Edification gains nothing from the exaggerations in the legend, which ends by making the most moving illustrations of the doctrine ridiculous".[77] Refraining from any more serious charge, we shall do well to keep this criticism in mind.[78]

The third point is this: on account of these very excesses the ideal forged by the Buddhist imagination ultimately becomes unrealisable. Even as early as the *Jataka* we find the being who is one day to be the Buddha Sakyamuni getting himself eaten by a tigress because she was so hungry that she was about to commit the colossal sin of devouring her own little ones. At another time, as a hare, he roasts himself to help a starving Brahman. There are many more stories of this kind. "This is all very fine, of course," remarks Fr. Allo,[79] "and no doubt we should not rise to such heights ourselves, but all the same these deeds seem to be chosen in such a way that it would be very unlikely for anyone to find himself in the position of having to imitate them." Furthermore, "this love of the colossal, and the passion for outbidding each other", passed from the illustrations into the rules themselves: nowhere is this more evident than in the Mahayanist teaching about the Paramitas, where it spoils the sublime ideal that was emerging. "It is not sufficient for a Bodhisattva to be charitable, virtuous, patient

and so on; he has to have an 'insatiable', or 'colossal' capacity
for charity, virtue, patience. To each creature he longs to give
persons 'as numerous as the sands of the Ganges', and give
them away every moment, for periods of time 'as numerous as
the sands of the Ganges', and so on."[80] By the ordinary law
a Bodhisattva must not eat without giving part of his food to the
destitute. This rule appears to have been too lenient for the
author of the *Ratnarasi*, for he tells the Bodhisattva to think of
the bacteria in his body and say to himself: "Inside me there
are eighty thousand legions of microbes. May they comfort
themselves with this food! At the moment I am providing for
their needs with meat; when I have attained to Illumination,
I shall provide them with Dharma."[81]

If, in the event, a real Bodhisattva happens to be involved,
he will have no difficulty in fulfilling the most colossal vows,
for the most miraculous achievements will be no more than
ordinary exercises for him:

> The Bodhisattva of the Body of the Law can transform
> himself in a twinkling into innumerable bodies and so
> render homage to the Buddhas of the ten districts; in a
> twinkling he can create immense riches and give them to
> other beings; harmonising sounds high, medium and low,
> he can in a twinkling preach the Law to all; and the Bod-
> hisattva continues these exercises until he is seated under the
> tree of Illumination. It is by this kind of exercise that the
> Bodhisattva of the Body of the Law practises the perfection
> of the virtue of giving [danaparamitaparipini].[82]

Faced with examples, rules, phantasmagoria like these, how
can one ever rise to such heights in actual practice? For the
modest Bodhisattva of flesh and flood only one method remained—that of symbolism.[83] All the actions of everyday life,
even the easiest and most common—opening or shutting a door,
sitting down, getting up, lying down, washing one's hands,
rinsing one's mouth—acquire an immense value if they are

performed with a view to the good "of all beings". Santideva, for example, says: "The thought of sacrificing all one possesses —and even the fruit of one's sacrifice—to all beings, is the perfection of charity. Charity is therefore entirely of the mind." This is pushing the moral aspect of intention a bit far. And such perfection is, moreover, ensured by a very simple kind of practice: the practice of parinamana or the "reverse effect" (Chavannes): "All the different good deeds which have been performed according to the three kinds of behaviour (by the body, by speech and by thought), and even all kinds of merit, such as those which come from repentance or exhortation or request or rejoicing in company, can return as benefits to the whole multitude of beings of the Dharmadatu, so that together they may have an intuition of Bodhi."[84] Thus, at the end of his learned *Treatise on the Demonstration of the Act*, Vasubandhu declares: "I wish to use my own merit to help others: may they all attain to the pure mind!"[85] No doubt this is an excellent practice, based on a principle similar to that underlying what we call the "treasury of merit", but it is a practice which can be made use of to avoid many kinds of heroism and even many duties. Finally, is there any more reality in the vow made by the Bodhisattva to be born again into "evil destinies", and even into the great hell of Avici, in order to draw sinners out of it?[86] This is certainly an heroic vow—all the more so as, according to at least one of the schools of the Great Vehicle, the day will never come when there is no great Avici, and no sinners. . . .[87] But the zeal which inspires such a vow is so great that, for the person who has determined upon it, the descent into Avici will be "like a walk in a pleasure garden".[88] There is no point in really trying to discover whether such zeal will do away with sorrow, or if it will simply enable joy to be found in suffering; in point of fact, it is highly unlikely that our Bodhisattva will ever arrive in any place that is to be feared, for his determination never to enter into nirvana whilst there are any sinners left to be liberated does not prevent him from having been in "the nirvana which is not entered" ever since the day on which he first became aware of this. And can the great Avici into which he intends to descend really be entered when he has already descended into the "nirvana which is not entered"?

Buddhism, it has been said, looks upon existence as a dream. It is certainly true that even at its best Buddhism is far too like a dream itself. "And the Word became flesh" is something no Buddhist will ever say. Compared with these lofty flights of imagination, which in practice are so utterly incapable of ensuring any consistent line of action, Our Lord's words may seem simple and even ordinary; but there is a firmly based historical authenticity in "Greater love hath no man than this, that a man lay down his life for his friends", and in dying on the Cross!

But we have not yet reached the heart of the matter. The essential thing, the thing that puts a gulf between Buddhist charity and Christian charity, is that in Christianity the neighbour is loved for himself. In Buddhism this is impossible. It is true that in both religions charity consists, at least in its early stages, in loving the other for himself; but since in Buddhism the ego is entirely illusory, or exists only to be destroyed, it can hardly be loved for itself. How, then, can anyone else's ego really be loved? Since it is not taken seriously, another's personality can never be the object of any serious love. "The insignificance of the individual is for the Buddhist a fundamental axiom, like the infinite value of the human soul for the Christian." This remark is made by Keyserling[89] in support of a hostile point of view, to the detriment of "the active love" of the Christian. It nevertheless states a truth, and one of capital importance. For this is why the loving-kindness of Buddhism, even when it manifests itself as tenderness towards creatures, is not properly translated by our word "charity". With certain reservations which we shall explain later, it remains essentially "pity" or "compassion". It is not, nor can it be, directed towards any being in himself, but only to his moral or physical sufferings. Now this could never be said of Christian charity, for this "never simply goes from rich to poor or from strong to weak or from the wise to the ignorant. It does not, in itself, assume any blemish or lack in the person receiving it".[90] It is quite true that in its highest manifestation on earth it appears as an immense compassion for the disinherited and an utter devotion to them; nevertheless, the condition always holds that in the very way in which it is exercised this devotion must proclaim the essential nobility of every human being and the essential unity of the whole human family. Not that pity is to be excluded![91] For a Christian, pity is "one of the overtones sounded by true love when struck with unhappiness", but it is not for all that the essence or the source of love. "Pity must grow from love; love cannot grow from pity";[92] in the admirable words of St. Augustine, "Do away with unhappiness, and there will be no further need for works of mercy. Will the fire of love be extinguished then?"[93]

Now Buddhist tenderness, even when manifested in action, even at its most sublime, never rises above pity. And if it often appears as true human tenderness, this is in spite of its doctrine. For the individual counts for little in Buddhism—so little, that this pity is declared to be all the more perfect, the more it becomes abstract and generalised; in other words, the less human it becomes. It is more concerned with suffering in general than with each suffering being in particular. "Put an end to sorrow", Sakyamuni used to say to his disciples; and this sorrow is the evil of existence itself—let us say, not to prejudge the issue, physical existence, at least—with all the evils arising from it; rather than the private griefs of the suffering "aggregates" of humanity. On this point there is no difference whatsoever between the two Vehicles. It is thus, for instance, that Santideva understands the matter: "I must," he says, "fight against the unhappiness of others as I do against my own, because it is unhappiness. . . . There is no subject to experience the unhappiness: who then can have

38

his own? All kinds of unhappiness without distinction are impersonal: they must be fought against as unhappiness. Why these restrictions?"[94] This is an idealist expression of a theme found throughout Buddhism. Such an argument, whilst its aim is to uproot the egoism in man and make him fight against the evil that afflicts others as well as that which afflicts himself, at the same time prevents any genuine concern for the sufferings *of others*. The being who suffers no more exists than the being who behaves wickedly or insultingly; and the thing that allows a man to remain calm under insults, without there being anything even to forgive, also enables him to exercise pity without being moved by any kind of misery whatever.[95]

This is the only conception of Buddhist pity which can be reconciled with the contemplative ideal professed by both the Mahayana and the Hinayana. For the difficulty appears at once: in the fully formed Bodhisattva, is not solicitude for others incompatible with that state of serenity or "impassive quietude" which constitutes the fourth degree of dhyana and in which he should be entrenched? To this Kumarajiva replies: "No, there is no incompatibility between these two things; for the person who desires the good of others does not envisage them in the concrete but in the abstract. He looks upon them, in fact, as a mirage or a dream, or the reflection of the moon in water, or the froth on the waves, or the echo of a sound, or the wake left by the flight of a bird. . . ."[96]

Some Western historians make a mistake here. Seeing quite clearly that Buddhist pity does not end with mere individuals and is not to be confused with any kind of facile sentimentality, they are inclined to take its generalised character as a sign of universality, forgetting that general and universal are as different as abstract and concrete. Some of these writers do at least realise that Christian charity is universal, and in their determination to glorify Buddhist pity they equate the two things; others, sharing the same error, see that Christian charity is directed towards human beings in all their particularity and conclude from this that it cannot be universal. And so they

contrast the two things; and when they contemplate the metaphysical heights in which Buddhist pity sits enthroned,[97] they
find Christian charity much inferior. The mistake which is
involved here will be realised more clearly when it is seen to
what degree Buddhism can push abstraction in this domain in
the Mahayanist theory of the three sorts of pity; for according
to this theory it is not sufficient for pity to be general, it must
end by being "empty".

The first sort of pity has as its object the beings who suffer;
it is sattvalambana karuna—the ordinary, inferior kind of pity,
tainted by the vulgar error of believing in the reality of living
beings. The second sort, which is higher, has as its object painful sensations in themselves; this is dharmalambana karuna, and
the person who experiences it knows that beings do not exist,
but only their Dharma.[98] But this is still only an approximation
to true knowledge, for the painful sensations do not exist in or
by themselves; and so this second sort of pity still involves
avidya (nescience). There must therefore be a third kind of
pity—pure pity, the pity which has no object: analambana
karuna. A virtue is all the higher, the more it is in this sense
pure. Perfect, ideal pity—"the great pity"—will therefore
arise, not from the love of creatures nor to put an end to suffering, but quite gratuitously, from the love of pity itself.[99] And,
at this highest level, just as it is no longer directed towards any
living being or any reality, so it is not the possession of any
particular person. "For the Mahayanist thinker, karuna is
universal but never anthropomorphic."[100] Only on this
condition can the giving which it inspires be "pure". Even
a person who sacrificed himself for all living beings in general,
in a spirit of complete disinterestedness, would still only be
performing a "worldly" action which could not lead him to the
desired end, if he still believed in the real existence of the people
for whom he was sacrificing himself or if he believed in his own
existence. But if he knows that there is "no person who gives,
nothing given, no person who receives the gift", then his gift
"involves no renunciation". He is at last pure and perfect.[101]

From this derive two further characteristics of Buddhist charity which finally serve to differentiate it from Christian charity. In the first place, it is a provisional virtue, not an absolute value; a means, not an end. And consequently the teaching which centres round it is an exoteric teaching which ultimately bears no reference to anything whatsoever.

It is a provisional virtue; in other words, it is still part of what Buddhists call "the mundane order". Not in terms of this virtue can the Supreme Being—or non-Being—be defined, nor can such a virtue enter into any account of man's last end. Here, as everywhere else in Buddhism, the absence of a real God, a living God, a God of charity, makes itself felt most painfully. For the Christian the commandment to love God is founded upon God's love for man, and this love of God for man expresses the very Being of God: *Deus est Caritas*. And the second commandment, the love of one's neighbour, is based on the first; it is like unto the first. For man was made in the image of God. But the first commandment, being based on God Himself, is eternal: it not only describes the way, it also suggests the end; besides being rule and means, it is object and reward. The same is true of the second commandment, which is like unto the first. Because of the divine image which lies at the heart of his being, in fact, every man, shares in the eternity of God. This resemblance lies at the root of his distinctive nature, and forms the fundamental solidity of his being.[102] *Solidabor in Te, Deus meus.*[103] Life eternal, therefore, will still demand the love of the neighbour, as it involves the love of God, for ever. Faith and hope will pass away, and give place to sight and possession, but charity will not pass away.[104]

Now there is nothing of this in Buddhism. Since in the depths of his being there is no ontological solidity deriving from a Creator; since he is nothing but a mass of component parts, with no inner unity, therefore there is nothing in the human being that can call for, or make possible, any ultimate love.[105] Altruism of any kind, whatever its tinge, and however ardent it may be, can only be a procedure for getting rid of desire.

To adopt a rather crude but expressive metaphor, "the purpose of a purge is evacuation, but it must also be evacuated itself, or else it will do more harm than good".[106] Buddhist charity is such a purge; that is to say, it is part of the technique of detachment. This is obviously true as regards the simple maitri of the Little Vehicle. It is also true for dana and karuna, as found in both the Little and the Great Vehicles. Max Scheler saw this clearly: "If Buddha accords any positive value to love, this is entirely because it means a 'redemption of the heart', not because it is a source of positive inspiration; and also because, whilst it has the 'incidental' effect of causing acts of charity and kindness, it supplies a technique which allows man to transcend his individual, self-enclosed ego and to liberate himself, at the very highest level of absorption, from his individuality and his personality in general. What Buddha considers valuable in love and in the techniques which derive from it, is the fact that it affords a starting-point, not that it leads to a particular end. In other words, the only thing he values in love is the detachment from self which it demands, the negation of self, the abandonment of self: these being conditions for which all other modes of being simply supply model 'pretexts'."[107]

One must also agree with Scheler that even the most ardent Mahayanist altruism is still, despite its appearance, "individualistic, indeed solipsist, because it derives its meaning, not from the efforts made by the lover to raise and strengthen the value of the beloved, but [from the efforts] at annihilation, at the suppression of the reality and mode of being of the lover". Marcel Granet hardly exaggerates therefore when he says that Buddhist charity consists in "freeing oneself from all the worldly vanities which are opposed to one's salvation and passing them on to others"[108]—which hardly means doing others a good service. The young prince Visvantara, the future Buddha Sakyamuni, certainly freed himself from fearful worldly ties when he abandoned, in turn, his goods, his children and his wife to the people who wanted them; but one pities those he benefited.

Charity is not the only virtue which helps to annihilate desire through the "extinction" of the ego, but its utilitarian and provisional character is emphasised by the place assigned to it in the list of Paramitas or Perfections. Mahayanist scholasticism includes six Paramitas, "summarizing the whole of the Great Vehicle": dana (giving), ciba (morality), ksanti (patience), virya (energy), samadhi (ecstasy), prajna (wisdom). The order is significant. This is how Asanga comments on it:[109]

> The Bodhisattva begins by working for others, by means of the first three Paramitas: by giving—i.e. performing acts of generosity; by morality—doing no evil; by patience—being tolerant. Then he works for himself by means of the next three Paramitas: from the foundation of Energy he directs his thought towards Ecstasy and finds deliverance through Wisdom . . .
>
> The six Paramitas are enunciated in this order because it is in this order that they lead to one another, becoming higher and higher and more and more refined . . .
>
> It is in this order that they lead to each other: having no concern for any kind of fortune, the Bodhisattva embarks upon morality, and so on. It is in this order that they get higher and higher: morality is higher than giving, and so on. It is in this order that they grow more and more refined: giving is, in fact, vulgar, and so on.

The Paramitas always appear in this order—in collections of edifying stories like the *Lieou tou tsi king* of Seng-houei (d. 280) translated by Edouard Chavannes,[110] in the early *Cariya Pitaka*, a Pali collection of *Jatakas*,[111] and again in the great *Treatise* by Nagarjuna. I do not see, incidentally, how an "hierarchic order" of the kind which Jean Thamar has tried to establish can possibly be accepted;[112] according to this, dana would occupy the fourth place, immediately in front of dhyana and prajna as "pre-eminently a mediating virtue". Not that this would in fact do anything to diminish the contrast which has always been maintained between "giving" and "wisdom".

Whether the giving be "mundane" or "supramundane", it is no doubt a "wonderful fruit loved by gods and men"; to the extent that it is practised, "the passions decrease", and hence it embodies "the first condition of nirvana". But in fact it is never more than the most elementary and remote condition. And Candrakirti is careful to tell us that dana, like the virtues which come after it, is never a Paramita except in a relative sense, the word Paramita only being properly used of prajna.[113] No doubt it is true that Nagarjuna, like many others, shows us Sakyamuni producing a thought of great loving-kindness (mahamaitrisitta) for the benefit of those who are in error, taking them by the hand of his great compassion and introducing them into the destiny of the Buddhas.[114] But this by no means reduces the significance of the fact I am insisting upon here; for it is then specifically stated that this dual state of mind is never to be confused with any human feeling, the person who exercises it experiencing in fact "no aversion or affection for anyone";[115] and whereas Jesus Christ dies in a supreme act of love, the greatest acts of charity which legend attributes to the Buddha are not considered worthy to figure in his final existence.[116]

In the doctrine of the Yogacaras there is a dual theory which can easily be misleading on this point. On the one hand, the Yogacaras say that the Buddhas draw beings towards themselves, that they work to bring them to "maturity" until they are capable of attaining to Buddhahood themselves. They then go on to say that the Buddhas, without waiting for this "maturity" to be fully realised, provide beings with a foretaste of supreme felicity by appearing to them through their sambhogakaya. But in fact neither of these theories has any connection at all with the Christian God of charity.

The first idea reminds one rather of Aristotle's unmoved and unloving God, from whom all beings are suspended by desire. Indeed, according to the explanation given by Asanga, "The Buddhas do not really say to each other, 'Here is one who is ready for me; here is one whom I have to help develop into maturity'; but it is the whole mass of beings, without any supreme Operator, which moves forward towards perfect maturity everywhere and in all places". And, moreover, the Buddhas themselves have no real being; they are simply aspects of an impersonal and unsubstantial Buddhahood which absorbs them all into one single Dharmakaya.[117] As for the second theory, this is the God of Spinoza or any other similar pantheist: an Absolute which needs relative beings to arrive at any consciousness of itself and whose manifestation to these relative beings is never, therefore, the result of charity; for at the root of charity lies, necessarily, independence. If the Buddhas are not satisfied with the Dharmakaya in which they are united, if they appear to the Bodhisattvas through the medium of their sambhogakayas, it is because their own interests are involved. "Neither the sun nor the moon, nor the surface of the water which is like a mirror, nor the light, is conscious of itself, but when three of these things are put in relation to each other, then an image is produced" (*Suvarna prabhasa sutra*). "What does this mean," Masson-Oursel comments, "if not that the Dharmakaya, symbolised by the sun or the moon, cannot take any delight in itself unless it is reflected by beings relatively but not absolutely different from itself—i.e. the Bodhisattvas, represented here by the mass of water—and that the intermediary uniting these two is sambhogakaya, which here appears as the light—a metaphor all the more suitable as from one point of view it really is a kind of meteor. Spinoza, discussing a similar problem but using different concepts, likewise declared that in the intellectual love of God, the love of man for God, the love of God for man, and the love of God for Himself, are one and the same thing."[118] But in that case there can be no question of any kind of charity.[119]

At first sight it might still be thought that there is in Buddhism something analogous to the Christian love of one's neighbour, based on the love of God, and to the Christian doctrine of man as a being made in the image of God. In the *Bodhicaryavatara* of Santideva appears the following:

> The creatures resemble the Buddhas in that they possess a share of the virtues of a Buddha . . .
>
> This tiny share is present in all creatures; it is because of its presence that all creatures are to be honoured.[120]

But this is only true in a relative sense, from a superficial point of view and by a merely utilitarian practice. When it comes to absolute truth, the Buddhas are unreal, and this sets a stamp of unreality upon the love of the neighbour which is founded upon their love.

This brings us to our final point. Buddhist charity, being provisional and not final, and remaining a means extrinsic to the end sought, vanishes inevitably when it is regarded from the point of view of absolute truth. Its teaching will always, therefore, be somewhat exoteric—if a doctrine about God was involved, we should say somewhat anthropomorphic. Here again it is in striking contrast to Christian charity. In His highest revelation, God revealed Himself as Love, and the learned doctors of Christianity have never been afraid to link this love with the most human feelings, rather than allow the realism of the revelation to be dimmed.[121] When we read the Gospels we find that the rule of brotherly love is its highest teaching: Christ insists on it at the end of His earthly life and leaves it as a legacy to His friends. After His death all the disciples insist on the supreme importance of this love; whilst the mystical asceticism of the most detached monks who ever lived was entirely subordinated to it.[122] Whereas if we open the Buddhist scriptures, this is the sort of thing we come across— in the story of Yasa, the young man of Benares who had grown tired of a life of pleasure and gone and joined the school of Buddha:

> When Yasa was seated near him, the Blessed One imparted to him, step by step, the teaching: first he instructed him in charity (dana), morality (sila), and the heavenly rewards (svarga); then in the misery, vanity and defilement of desire, and the happiness gained by renouncing it.[123]

And when, after meditating on these truths, Yasa has reached the stage of being able to understand more, Sakyamuni imparts to him "the teaching which is special to the Buddhas"; and this includes absolutely nothing at all, even in its earliest stages, about charity.[124]

This characteristic of the Buddhist scriptures is emphasised by all their writers. "Generosity is preached to beginners," writes Aryadeva,[125] "vows to the semi-advanced, and the void to the advanced." Like Christ, in fact—and even more so—"the Buddha preaches the Law according to the needs of beings".[126] The principle of "economy" thus occupies an important place in Buddhist teaching, a place even more important than it does in the Christian revelation.[127] But its values are inverted.

The Bodhisattva, therefore, practises a dual kind of perfection: the perfection of giving and the perfection of knowledge (Danaparamita and Prajnaparamita). These, as we have seen, are the first and the last in the graduated series of Paramitas. But the first is not only, as in the instruction given by the Buddha himself, entirely subordinated to the last, which is the one and only "matrix of Buddhahood" (Tathagatagarbha); it is absorbed into it and disappears. For charity has no value except from a purely relative point of view; it needs to be supported by the "particular imagination which brings out relative characteristics", as certain illnesses cause spots before the eyes.[128] Even when it is purified, therefore, it rests upon an illusion—an illusion in which, no doubt, there is no harm, and even a great deal of use, but which must in the end be dissipated to give place to the establishment of the Void and the absolute indifference which results from this. In actual fact, for the person who has attained to the perfection of knowledge there is no kind of sympathy or antipathy left: these are both "disturbances", which have been exorcised for ever. "Good and evil, mother or prostitute, are in his eyes identical." All the Dharma are equal and all are equally empty.[129]

We shall not be surprised to find, therefore, that the classic meditation "on the four sublime feelings", as given for example in the *Mahasudassanasutta*, rises from love and mounts by way of pity and joy to serenity. Nor shall we be surprised to discover Nagarjuna, the author of the *Mahaprajnaparamitasastra*, the first great *Summa* of the Mahayana, declaring that "without Prajnaparamita, Danaparamita would be classed amongst the perishable Dharma of the world, or"—and this is hardly less contemptuous, coming from an apostle of the Great Vehicle— "would simply end in the Parinirvana of the Arhats and the Pratyeka Buddhas";[130] nor to find Asanga ending his famous work, the *Mahayanasutralamkara*, with two chapters on Conduct and Judgment, in which, after describing the Compassion of Buddha, he praises the state of indifference in which the Buddha is finally installed, "without conflict, without need, without disturbance";[131] nor to come across a sudden change of tone in the voice of Santideva, the greatest poet of Bodhisattvic charity. The passages quoted above were taken from the first songs of the *Bodhicaryavatara*, but in the ninth song, which is dedicated to Wisdom, the voice of charity is silent and the whole universe is denounced as an illusion. Charity was part of the world of appearances; henceforward the Bodhisattva will accustom himself to the only "real" world, the universal Void. "'The whole procession of virtues' unfolded in the first eight songs 'has as its object Wisdom', said the saint." Wisdom alone will put an end to sorrow. But to obtain Wisdom it must first be understood that there are two truths—veiled truth, and absolute truth; to which correspond two kinds of men—the ordinary man and the contemplative. The Wisdom of the contemplative is acquired by a subtle process of initiation into the doctrine of the Void. Santideva discusses this, then he returns briefly to the first stage, which he explains in the following words:

Just as the trunk of the banana tree, when it has disintegrated into its various parts, no longer exists, so the Ego, when studied critically, is recognised to be pure nothingness.

If the individual does not exist, on what can compassion be exercised? The individual is imagined by an illusion which has been adopted because of the aim in view. Whose aim, since the individual does not exist? It is true that the effort derives from illusion, but as the aim is the smoothing away of sorrow, therefore, though it is an illusion, it is not forbidden.[132]

When the time comes, however, we must learn to free ourselves from this illusion: "The destiny of beings is like a dream . . . Understand, my brothers, that everything is void, like space."[133]

Just as, in its aspiration towards nirvana, Buddhism, in spite of its negations, has sometimes had a presentiment of the true God, so in its apostolic longings, of which there are so many signs in the Mahayana, it has had a presentiment of true Charity. We may say, in fact, that at its best Buddhist charity resembles Christian charity as a dream resembles reality.[134] The great Bodhisattvas of charity are like remote, floating, unreal prefigurings of the Christ, not creatures of flesh and blood like the saints of the Church; but the mere fact of having imagined them, even in dream, is far too profound and noble an achievement not to be worthy of admiration. Meditating in front of the "fine Bodhisattva" in the cave at Ajanta, Philippe Stern observes that through the face there shines a soul "at once offered and withdrawn"—"infinite peace, cut off from the world and its noise in a state of perfect recollection, at one with itself and with charity, and with compassion for the entire universe." The two extremes, of offering and withdrawal, seem to meet. "Uniting these two extremes, the Bodhisattva seems entirely withdrawn into himself in a state of infinite calm, isolating himself from the world to attain to the deepest levels that lie beyond him, and opening outwards towards the world in an overflow of self-giving."[135] This description is not by any means idealised; but (we must remember) it is a description of a dream.

Maitri, as it appears in the reality of history and human relationships, is a more moderate virtue, but it is nevertheless one
of great charm. Buddhist loving-kindness and gentleness are
better qualities than certain tactless kinds of zeal and busy-
bodying "charity". One of the weaknesses of the humanism
that derives from maitri, however, is that it cannot ultimately
have any respect for the personality of others.[136] More deeply,
perhaps, it must be charged with failing to understand both
the strength and the uncompromising quality of love, and the
profound nature of the "mysterious, total gift of self". It must
also be charged with lacking fundamentally in justice. These
criticisms are sometimes made against Christian charity
through a lack of understanding of its nature, but of Buddhist
charity they seem to be thoroughly justified.[137] Maitri, a love
without affection, takes on a kind of emotional tinge in karuna,
which in its turn becomes effective as dana; to what extent,
we have tried to show. But the more charity is realised in this
way, the more it becomes a mere means. Dana is never anything but provisional; even at its most sublime it is simply a
form of almsgiving; whilst karuna tends towards abstraction
and pure gratuitousness: it is ultimately pity without an object.
Finally, maitri retains a cerebral element even in its highest
form; its smile is always, so to speak, a little enigmatic. In the
end, no matter what may be said about sambhoga,[138] there is
no unitive charity, no reciprocity—nor can there be: because
there are no beings to give themselves to each other. Unity is
only achieved through impersonality.

As it is untrue to say—as a great many Westerners have said
—that the Buddhist nirvana signifies nothingness, so is it untrue
that maitri, with its sequence of altruistic virtues, is purely
negative—as is proved indeed by its results. "One has to
think back," says René Grousset,[139] "to the grim pre-Columbus
civilisations of North America, where one seeks in vain from
beginning to end for any smile of humanity or breath of
tenderness, to understand what Asia owes to the First Sermon
of Benares." And no doubt this is why the same author, despite

his intimate knowledge of Christian doctrine, can speak today, as Burnouf did in his day, of "Buddhist charity".[140] Nevertheless, it is as true of maitri as it is of nirvana that its positive value never manages to extricate itself and emerge in all its fullness.[141] Whereas Christ came to light the fire of love upon earth, Buddha simply aims to extinguish "the fire of hatred, desire and ignorance" (Mahavagga). Whereas the culminating point of history and the world is found, by Christians, on Calvary, the centre of the Buddhist universe is the Tree of Buddha Gaya—and the Bodhi-Tree and the Tree of the Cross, though they are both "cosmic Pillars", are entirely different in essence. Instead of the penetrating analysis of love that we find for instance in St. Augustine, St. Bernard, Fénelon, Buddhism offers us speculations on the Void,[142] which reach their highest pitch of rarification in the Great Vehicle:

> Emptiness is like the space of the sky
> In which can be seen anything that appears . . .
> Whatever comes into sight,
> Do not believe in it but let it go:
> This is the rule that has been given
> To keep Bodhi in one's hand . . .
> The appearance not hiding the Emptiness,
> The Emptiness not annihilating the appearance.[143]

It would be a mistake to attempt to account for these contrasts by saying that they are merely the results of differences in point of view or of the degree of depth reached in the critique of knowledge. Many Christian thinkers have shown considerable boldness in rejecting appearances and establishing a scientific "negative theology", and the most classic and authoritative of them have often proved the boldest. In Christianity, nevertheless, affirmation always triumphs in the end. If this is not true of Buddhism, it is because it lacks the only possible Foundation: God, creative Love. All the insufficiency—all the falsity, in fact—of the Buddhist religion, comes in the final analysis from this. The failure of this tremendous adventure—the foundering of this gigantic raft on which half humanity embarked for Deliverance—came about because the Buddha was ultimately unable to see beyond the divinities of mythology and popular animism to the face of the God of Charity.

The Law which he believed he had found—"a profound Law, difficult to fathom, difficult to understand"[144]—is itself, in the end, illusion. He was not able to utter the liberating word. We should not criticise him unduly. More than any other man who has ever lived, perhaps, he grasped the problem of human destiny, and led a whole *pars purificans* towards the good, for which Christians too can be grateful to him. He avoided the deceptive ways—always so tempting—of superstition, automatic asceticism, gnosis. He saw the need for a spiritual deprivation beyond the night of the senses. No doubt he failed to achieve his aim. Without the "fullness" of charity no one will ever realise the "void" of detachment. Without the "yes", which can only be a reply, the necessary "no" cannot, finally, be uttered. "It is not through self that one escapes from self". Even though the Buddha's doctrine, in spite of its tone of profound humanity, is inhuman in its rigour, and even though, as history has abundantly shown, it was fatally subject to the most dreadful corruptions, it does not appear any the less profound or logical—or indeed inevitable, so long as the personal Idea was missing, the divine Word, Jesus Christ, by whom today we live.

TWO COSMIC TREES

THE famous Buddhist stupa at Sanchi is the only building of ancient India which remains in a state of perfect preservation. This it may owe to its being situated at a considerable distance from the main invasion-routes followed by Islam. The sculptures on its four gateways (torana) which face the four points of the compass, supply material of the utmost value for our knowledge of ancient Buddhism. The only part which concerns us at the moment, however, is the outside face of the left pillar at the northern gateway.

On this there is inscribed a most peculiar design. At the top is a vardhanana—made up of a cakra (circle) and a trisula (trident)—surmounted by a chattra (the umbrella of royalty), much reduced in size. Underneath these, running down either side, as though down a tree-trunk, are two rows of little palm-branches bearing garlands of precious stones. Right at the bottom there are two paduka (footprints), each marked with a cakra.[1] The general meaning of this figure cannot be doubted: it is a symbolical representation of the Buddha. From the fact that the feet are not seen from in front but are rather the prints or traces of feet, Gilbert Combaz concludes that the whole thing could be regarded as a symbol of "the way to be followed": "We should thus have an expression of the *Dhammapada*, the way of Dharma." Nevertheless, he himself is not content with this explanation, for in fact the feet do not exist on their own: the whole figure inevitably suggests that some person is being symbolised.

Not of course a merely human individual; not the Buddha Sakyamuni in his mere individuality, even though magnified by the royal attribute of the chattra. To the cakra which represents the head there is joined the trisula—the "Three Jewels", the emblem of the three elements composing the whole of Buddhism; Buddha, Dharma, Sangha. When amplified in this way, our character with his trunk of palm-branches and jewels can be identified with two further things, which together make up a unique and highly complex symbol. On the one hand the monument turns out to be a pillar; and this pillar surmounted by a cakra (i.e. the face of the sun) is without any doubt at all the cosmic pillar, the meeting place of north, south, east and west, the sun's axis at its zenith, the prop of the universe whose base rests on the earth and whose summit reaches to the sky. On the other hand, it is no less certainly a tree, a sacred tree, the tree of life, a symbol of universal fertility and everything that is truly valuable. Thus, this sculpture on the north torana at Sanchi presents us with a man, a tree and a pillar, so closely united that they have become one. The Buddha, when considered in his highest essence, is at once the Cosmic Pillar and the Tree of Life. [2]

As is known, a great deal of light has been shed on the iconography of Romanesque and Gothic churches by Emile Mâle, who has studied this iconography with reference to the writings which originally inspired it. Now it so happens that one of the texts which best facilitate our study of the Buddhist sculpture is a Christian text, a passage taken from a homily on Easter, which figures amongst the *spuria* of St. John Chrysostom. Fr. Charles Martin, who has studied this text at length, holds it to be the treatise by St. Hippolytus on Easter that is mentioned by Eusebius in his *History of the Church*. This has recently been challenged, first by Dom Connolly and then by Pierre Nautin, on what seem to be fairly solid grounds. [3] Here, in any case, in translation, is the passage which concerns us. It occurs in a description of the Cross:

This wood is provided for my salvation . . . I establish myself in its roots, I lay myself down under its branches . . .

Under its shade I set up my tent . . . Its fruit provides me with perfect joy . . . This tree goes up from the earth into the heavens; it is the plant of immortality, rising in the middle of heaven and earth—the firm prop of the universe, joining all things together, the support of the whole inhabited earth, twining the cosmos together and including in itself the whole medley of human nature. Nailed down by the invisible nails of the Spirit, so that he will never waver in his fidelity to the divine, touching the sky with the crown of his head, establishing the earth with his feet, and in the space between heaven and earth embracing the innumerable spirits of the earth with his immeasurable hands . . ."[4]

It will be noticed how the Cross is here first compared to a tree, then to a cosmic support, finally to the Crucified One Himself. Nor are these comparisons arbitrary: they form a united whole. Thus it is Christ Himself who, on the Cross, is for us the tree of life and joy, whilst at the same time He is the nexus and prop of the whole universe. *Ego sum Vita . . . Omnia in Ipso constant.*

Neither the figure on the pillar at Sanchi nor the description by the Christian homilist is ἅπαξ: in both Christianity and Buddhism there is a whole tradition of ideas and works of art which could be drawn upon, if necessary, to elucidate them.

In Buddhism, for instance, there are many pillars set at the gates that lead to a stupa, which are surmounted by a cakra or a trisula—at Bharhut, for instance, at Mathura and at many places in Gandhara;[5] whilst in "The Lotus of the Good Law"[6] the Buddhas are said to be "like columns of gold" (suvarnayupa). The stupas themselves, which are symbolic burial mounds, or rather shrines, to the Buddha, are more than this; they are veritable "funeral corpses of the Buddha", veritable "bodily substitutes for the Buddha". (This is why they can without any impropriety be empty, i.e. in practice full, without any chamber of relics.) They are said to contain a pillar, which appears at the top with its harmika and umbrellas. Now this harmika, the abode of the gods, is at the summit of Mount Meru (or Sumeru), the cosmic mountain which rises up in the middle of the earth; it is arranged in tiers inside the stupa round the axis formed by the pillar. The secret chamber containing the Buddha himself in the guise of a few relics also contains, therefore—it is the same thing—the Cosmic Pillar. At the same time it contains—and this again is the same thing—the Cosmic Tree, which according to Buddhist ideas is essentially the tree of knowledge, enlightenment, omniscience. This is explained in a passage in the *Mahavamsa*,[7] describing the installation of such a tree, made of gold and precious stones, in the middle of a mahastupa. At Nepal some of the harmikas are decorated with eyes: these are the eyes of Adi-Buddha, whose head becomes one with the top of the pillar. In some parts of Indo-China eyes are represented on the stupa itself.[8] Thus Buddhist architecture presents us with the same symbol as Buddhist sculpture—a symbol more telling still in the Far East, where the dome of the stupa is left out, leaving its internal anatomy, so to speak, its skeleton, naked; the "vault of heaven" which enveloped the world having disappeared, there remains only the axis, the central pillar, with its tiers or storeys rising like a series of umbrellas.[9]

Sakyamuni, as is well known, received his enlightenment whilst he was meditating under a fig-tree (asvattha), after imbibing the food which he had received from Sujata in a golden bowl. This "unique fig-tree" (eka asvattha) from which Buddhist monasteries still make it their proud duty to cultivate a shoot even today—this "Bodhi-Tree" represents the Buddha himself, just as the stupa or cakra does. The asvattha appears frequently in the art of the early centuries. No doubt even before Sakyamuni is portrayed as a person, the tree often appears separate from him: at Bharhut, for example, and again at Amaravati, there is an altar or throne in front of the tree and footprints on the ground. These are transitional forms, until finally, in the last product of the Indian Buddhist schools, there remains only a tiny sprig of foliage decorating the Buddha's halo. But on the oldest monuments there is, properly speaking, no such dissociation. Some of the asvatthas, profusely decorated with little flowers and garlands, are decked out with jewels and surmounted by an umbrella as signs of the royal power of the victorious Buddha, and it was certainly as a direct substitute of the Buddha that the Emperor Asoka regarded these trees. Later, when an attempt was made to justify the substitution of the human form for the fig-tree, the order given by Sakyamuni to his disciple Sariputra was quoted. Sariputra had asked the Buddha in what form he should be venerated after his parinirvana, and the Buddha replied: "O Sariputra, when I have departed, my image should be cut in the shape of a fig-tree".[10] In the *Mahasukhavativyuha*, one of the works upon which Amidism is based,[11] and again in "The Lotus of the Good Law", one of the fundamental books of the Great Vehicle,[12] those who follow the Buddhas along the way of enlightenment are compared with large or small trees. The Sukhavati—which is the "Pure Land", the paradise of the Buddha Amitayus (or Amitabha)—is full of trees, made of gems and precious stones, that no doubt represent the various degrees of illumination.

There are other symbolical representations, identical with that which is to be found on the torana at Sanchi. Amongst the reliefs at Amaravati, dating from the last Andhras (second century A.D.), is a series of "Pillars of Fire" which are also Buddhas: instead of a head, there is a trisula; right at the bottom are feet marked with a wheel, resting on a lotus; and on each side of the column running through the middle of the pillar, instead of garlands of jewels, there are sparks of fire. Some of these columns are spirals, to symbolise the mounting of the flames; at the top, the trisula is either surrounded or surmounted by a "halo", again made of flame.[13] There is no difficulty in understanding the symbolism behind these monuments. We know from elsewhere that though the energy of fire (tejas) is present everywhere, it is present to a special degree in the Arhats, and, more especially still, at a maximum

57

of concentration, in the Buddha; from the *Theragata*[14] we know that this energy is the flaming sword of knowledge (prajna) with which Sakyamuni overcame the assaults of Mara; then there is the *Dhammapada*,[15] which the Buddha "burns with the energy of fire" (tapati tejasa). The Pillars of Fire at Amaravati represent this idea, developing it still further in a most striking relief: the Buddha becomes entirely assimilated to the element of Fire which is present as a secret source of energy in all forms of existence.

Finally, it should be remembered that the holy place of Buddhism, Buddha Gaya, the spot on which the Bodhi-Tree rises, is looked upon both as a mountain[16] and as the centre of the world; and this reinforces the symbolism of the Pillar.

Christian tradition possesses similar kinds of symbolism. In the first centuries of the Church, Christ was frequently represented as a giant whose head reached to the heavens or even towered above them—as in the *Gospel of Peter*,[17] the *Acts of John*,[18] the *Shepherd of Hermas*,[19] and so on.[20] St. Ambrose speaks of the *gigas geminae substantiae* (the giant with the dual nature).[21] The same gigantic proportions are attributed to Adam in the Rabbinical writings.[22]

Again, according to an old legend found in the *Apocalypse of Moses*, the *Gospel of Nicodemus* and the *Life of Adam and Eve*,[23] and recorded in the Middle Ages by Honorius of Autun[24] and again in our own day by Paul Claudel,[25] the Cross of the Saviour was made from the wood of the tree of good and evil. It is a tree itself, the Tree of Life—according to the words of the Apocalypse (xxii. 2): *lignum vitae . . . et folia ligni ad sanitatem gentium*.[26] This theme is "one of the oldest and most widely found" in the Christian tradition. It appears in innumerable passages, such as this from Gregory of Elvira, which echoes one of the ideas in our Homily on Easter:

. . . this tree showed clearly, like an image of the Cross, which to some appeared rough and harsh on account of its wood, but which supplied others with cooling shade. In truth, the faithful are protected by it from the heat of the fire of persecution, they are refreshed by it according to the words of the Scriptures: "I shall hope in the shadow of thy wings, until iniquity has passed away".[27]

Hence, no doubt, "the crosses covered with flowers, which divide the ceilings of some of the chambers in the Catacombs";[28] hence also, the rough crosses like trunks of palm-trees, as found, for instance, on the *ampullas* at Monza, and all the rustic crosses of the same kind which are to be found right up to the time of the Baroque period; the crosses shaped like the Tree of Life that can be seen on Romanesque baptismal fonts or under the burial porches (known as "paradises") of so many old churches; the crosses painted green, so common in the Middle Ages. There is also the well-known cross covered with gems and flowers in the baptistery at St. Pontian. In the psalter belonging to Robert de Linderey, Abbot of Peterborough (d. 1222) there is a picture of the Crucifixion in which the Cross is made of two trunks decorated with leaves and flowers.[29]

Now this cross, which is a tree, is sometimes Christ as well— "this living Cross which is the Body of the Redeemer", as Paul Claudel was to say.[30] For Christ—more precisely Christ on the Cross—is Himself the Tree of Life, planted in the middle of the Church which He feeds with His fruit, i.e. His own substance, as the first tree of life was planted in the middle of the Garden of Eden. He is Himself the Fruit of the tree, as used to be sung in the Middle Ages:

> *O crux, frutex salvificus,*
> *Vivo fonte rigatus,*
> *Cujus flos aromaticus*
> *Fructus desideratus . . .*

There comes to mind, too, the hymn by Fortunatus, which is still always sung during Holy Week:

Crux fidelis, inter omnes arbor una nobilis,
Nulla silva talem profert, fronde, flore, germine.
Dulce lignum, dulces clavos, dulce pondus sustinet.

Even in as early a work as the *Acts of Peter* it is said: "It is fitting to attach oneself to the Cross of Christ, which is the one vast and only Word . . . In this way the Word will be the upright part of the Cross on which I [Peter] am crucified."[31] This is a passage as remarkable as it is beautiful. Again and again Origen remarks that "the Scriptures describe Christ as a tree".[32] Similarly, St. Gregory of Nyssa says: "Solomon calls the Tree of Life, Wisdom, which is the Lord".[33] Many others say the same thing—for instance, St. Augustine,[34] Ambrose Autpert,[35] Duns Scotus,[36] Rupert of Deutz.[37] Honorius of Autun, as was his habit, included this traditional symbol in his collection: "The Tree of Life is Wisdom, the life of souls; this Tree, this wood, is Christ . . . or rather, the Cross which bears Christ—the Cross, bearing the Fruit of life. Christ is rightly compared to a tree, etc."[38] This helps to explain the symbolism of the mosaic discovered a short time ago in the baptistery of Henchir Messaouda, as described by Henri-Charles Puech in the *Cahiers archéologiques* for 1949: the Tree of Life which is to be seen there is a "complex image which refers at one and the same time to the paradisal condition to which the Christian is restored through baptism, to the living fruit of renewal gained through communion with the flesh of the Saviour and to the wood of the Cross of the Redemption; it is thus synonymous with the achievement of Christ and with Christ Himself".[39] Hence also those curious "living crosses", one of which can be seen in a fresco at Brüneck in the Tyrol (late sixteenth century), and also at the museum in Beaune (French School, seventeenth century): the arms of the cross are not only covered with branches (living on the right, dead on the left); they end in two human arms, the right arm crowning the Church, the left cleaving asunder the Synagogue; two other arms are grafted on to the head and foot of the cross, one opening the gate of heaven, the other breaking down the gates of hell.[40]

A similar, indeed an identical symbol is that of the Sacred Ladder, which is obviously, from its reference to Genesis, Jacob's Ladder. This symbol was very popular in the Syrian tradition. "Christ on the Cross," says James of Sarugh,[41] "stood on the earth, as on a ladder of many rungs." The West was not unaware of this symbol: even more significant for our purpose is a passage in an old Swedish missal which contains this prayer to Christ, to be said at the moment of the adoration of the Cross: "Lead us as by a ladder to heavenly things".[42] And St. Catherine of Siena, in one of her visions, likewise contemplates Christ as a bridge set up between heaven and earth.[43] Naturally, this ladder or bridge, which is Christ, stands at the centre of the earth, and from earth to heaven there is no other way except through this centre, for Christ on the Cross is the sole Mediator between man and God. This is also the meaning of the symbol of the mountain, of which St. Augustine says: "And what is this mountain by which we rise if not the Lord Jesus Christ?"[44]

This Ladder, which is at once the Cross and Christ, is also sometimes a column, a pillar—as in this hymn of St. Ephraim for the Feast of the Epiphany, alluding to the Baptism of Jesus:

Brothers, open your senses and contemplate the column, hidden in the air, whose base rests upon the waters and which reaches to the gate of the heights like the ladder seen by Jacob.

Upon this the light descended at the baptism and the soul is mounted up into heaven, so that we may be united in one single love.[45]

Like the Buddha on the monuments at Amaravati, Christ in the *Acts of Philip* is described as a "Pillar of Fire".[46] His disciples can share this privilege. Thus, in the *Apocalypse of Bartholomew*, Christ says to Andrew, blessing him: "Thou shalt be a column of light in the heavenly Jerusalem."[47] In a Mozarabic manuscript dating from the eleventh century and containing "the old Latin account of the Assumption", the Apostle Paul, invited by Peter to stand up and begin the prayer, replies: "How could I be the first to pray, since thou art a column of light?"[48] Some of the accounts found in writings of the old Coptic monastic tradition—the *Life of Abbot Pisentius*[49] is an example—show the spiritually perfect as being, like Christ, like God in the burning bush, Pillars of Fire joining heaven and earth.[50] Soon Manicheism, in which many Buddhist and Christian elements intermingled, was to define "the perfect man" as "the Pillar of Glory",[51] and later Jewish speculation was to identify Jacob's Ladder with the "central Pillar" where the mysterious Shekina resides.[52]

Finally, the passage from St. Hippolytus (if he in fact was its author) is only one amongst many in which the Cross is referred to explicitly as the axis and prop of the world, the nexus of the whole creation, the solid pillar around which the four quarters of the universe are arranged and organised. One of the most significant passages comes from Firmicus Maternus in his *De Errore Profanarum Religionum*:

> . . . Mankind is nourished and the whole world held together by an arm of this symbol [the Cross], which stretches out straight and perpendicular: while the east is influenced and the west sustained by their contact with the two arms which go out from its sides, so that the foundations of the whole world, which have been thus strengthened threefold, are held in place by imperishable roots . . . Thou, Christ, with hands stretched forth to the world, dost support the kingdom of heaven; our salvation hangs on Thine eternal shoulders . . . Wherefore, the wood of the Cross controls the movements of the heavens, renews the roots of the earth and leads to salvation those of us who cleave to it.[53]

The same thing is found again in St. Ambrose:

Just as the heavens are divided into four parts, north and south, east and west, so are they contained in the four points of the Cross [54]

and in St. Jerome:

What is the shape of the Cross, if not a four-cornered outline of the universe? The east shines forth from the top; the right arm signifies the north; the south corresponds with the left arm: the west is formed by the base. [55]

One finds the same thought expressed in St. Augustine, [56] St. Maximus of Turin, [57] St. Andrew of Crete, [58] and in many others. [59] It is naturally particularised and reinforced by the belief which we mentioned earlier when discussing the spot where the Buddhist tree of enlightenment stands: Calvary, where the Cross rises on the site of Adam's tomb, and from which life flows as it formerly flowed from the four rivers of the Garden of Eden, [60] was considered in the old Christian tradition, which in this inherited the Jewish tradition, [61] as the centre of the world. [62] Part at least of this symbolism has passed into a poem composed by Florus of Lyons in the ninth century on the occasion of the installation of certain martyrs' relics under the high altar in the Cathedral of St. John:

. . . Jerusalem, which shines forth with the Lamb, living and resplendent, sends out the four rivers of paradise from one source. [63]

And even today, on the day of the Exaltation of the Holy Cross, the Byzantine liturgy sings of "the Tree of Life planted on Calvary, the Tree on which the King of all the ages achieved our salvation", the Tree which, "rising up from the depths of the earth", "stands at the centre of the earth" and "sanctifies to the furthest bounds of the universe". "O surpassing miracle," it exclaims, "the length and breadth of the Cross stretch as far as the heavens!" [64]

The remarkable analogy which, as we began by noting, exists between the sculpture on a Buddhist pillar and a passage from a Christian homily, is thus simply a particularly striking example of a whole series of analogies. Are we to believe that this raises the question of any sort of inter-dependence?

We must note first of all that the idea behind the pillar at Sanchi is only a Buddhist variation of a number of older Indian ideas dating back to considerably earlier than Sakyamuni. There are many traces of it in Buddhist literature too. In an earlier existence the Bodhisattva had become a yaksa, i.e. the spirit of a tree. One *Jataka* tells us of a certain tree that formed the object of a cult: the five twigs which came out at the end of each of its branches were arranged, apparently, like the fingers of a hand.[65] On the balustrade of the stupas at Bharhut and Buddha-Gaya there can still be seen "a forked tree" (*eugenia jambotana*) out of which come two arms presenting a ewer and a dish to a person who at Bharhut is sitting on the ground and at Buddha Gaya is standing. This scene has been identified by Coomaraswamy with the one in the *Jataka* about the Treasurers, the Monks and the Spirit of the Tree. A number of monks who were returning from the Himalayas sat down under a banyan-tree, and one of them desired the spirit of the tree to give them food and drink and then a bath. The spirit eventually appeared to them, and all their requests were granted—as suggested in the concise manner indicated above."[66] Elsewhere it is related that the Bodhisattva, having gone down one day to bathe in the river Nairanjana, could not get back onto the bank without the help of a yaksa. At Amaravati there are "two sculptures representing this scene: one without any human figure in it and another in which the Bodhisattva is suggested by his feet only, but in the foliage of the tree can be seen the helping hand of the dryad stretched out towards the saint".[67] In the *Mahavamsa* it is said that when Sakyamuni wished to go amongst the Nagas where a war was imminent, he was accompanied on his journey by the yaksa of the tree Rajayatana in the garden Jatavana, which used its foliage as an umbrella to protect the Blessed One;[68] and according to the *Lalitavistara*, when the time of Bodhi arrived the eight divinities of the tree began to sing the praises of the future Buddha.[69]

The truth is that the tree with which Sakyamuni was identified by the faithful had long been venerated on the spot which was to become the Buddha Gaya: it was the tree nyagarodha, "the famous Aksaya-vata", to which people went on pilgrimage in search of immortality.[70] Indian folk-lore provides us with many similar cases: trees with which the figure of a woman is intertwined, as a symbol of the union between the human race and the sacred forces of nature; and (at a rather later period) divinities whose hands, arms, face or head and shoulders appear through the leaves of the tree, as in the scene on the bank of the river Nairanjana.[71]

These of course are chiefly examples of popular local cults, but if we consult the classic tradition of India we shall find others which are even more significant. The Tree of Life, the Cosmic Tree, is a frequent theme in the Vedas and Upanishads.[72] This Tree, synonymous with the whole of existence, the whole of life, stretches throughout space, from top to bottom; it has its root in the navel of the Supreme Being (Varuna, Mahayaksa, Brahman); it is the image and manifestation of this Being, the emanation of its Energy, the respiration of its Breath; it is the symbol of hidden deity; the greatest of the gods reveal themselves as the spirit moving its branches formed of all the elements—air, fire, water, earth . . . "This everlasting fig-tree," says the *Katha Upanishad*, "whose roots are in the air and its branches below, is the pure one, the Brahman, that which is called the undying. All the worlds rest upon it, nothing happens outside it".[73] Similarly, in the *Maitri Upanishad* the whole world is woven upon the Brahman, the gigantic tree, "the unique fig-tree", "the only Awakener", in which resides the fiery energy of the sun; pushing its branches into space in all directions, it spreads everywhere like a contemplative vision . . .[74]

65

Again, the god of fire, Agni, is conceived in the *Rig-Veda*[75] as the Pillar that supports men and gods and rules and protects the firmament; the axial tree of the Chariot of the Sun that separates and at the same time unites heaven and earth. The *Atharva-Veda* sings the praises of this Pillar "in which every existence is fixed":[76]

> Borne by it, heaven and earth stand firm. On it rests everything that has a soul, everything that breathes and sleeps . . . Ancient is its name, vast its idea. This whole universe is founded upon it, on it rests whatever moves and breathes . . . the great mystery at the centre of the world, to it all its vassals bring their tribute . . . whoever could know this Thread upon which all creatures are woven, would know the great Exegesis . . .

This unique Tree, this Pillar, this "Column of Gold",[77] this Axis of the world, is the stake of sacrifice which carries to the gods the offerings made by men and in this way ensures the regular progress of the universe (even before the sacrifice is itself raised to the rank of supreme divinity). It is a stake octagonal in shape, like some of the pillars of the Buddhist stupas discovered in Ceylon.[78] It is erected on the holy ground to the singing of: "Rise, O Lord of the forest, to the summit of the earth".[79] The name "Lord of the forest" emphasises its vegetable character, but it is also identified with Prajapati, the mythical ancestor of the world and humanity—or, rather the divine substance, in human form, of which they are made. For the three worlds which compose the entire universe, the spiritual, the heavenly and the earthly (svar, bhumas, bhin), are the three elements that constitute the very body of Prajapati.[80] Hence here again Buddhism appears as the heir to a tradition: if the body of the Buddha sums up in its three parts the whole universe, it is in this no more than a replica of the body of Prajapati as conceived in Brahman mythology.[81]

It seems reasonable to conclude from these various examples, therefore, that "the pre-Buddhist tradition lent itself to a kind of representation that was personal . . . but not anthropomorphic", and that "Buddhist artists did not fail to take advantage of this".[82] This being so, our question should now be formulated in more general terms: does our Christian homily depend in any way on the Indian ideas which are sufficient to account for the sculpture at Sanchi?

Even when the question is phrased in these wider terms, any conclusion would still be premature, for it should be noted that the identification of the Body of Christ with the Cross follows naturally from the identification of Christ with the Tree of Life. Now this latter identification can be explained without much difficulty. As has been intimated in some of the traditional passages quoted above, it is simply an application of an idea in Proverbs, iii. 18: Wisdom "is a tree of life to them that lay hold on her". For the Jews this wisdom was the Law;[83] for the Christians, the Son of God. The Christian interpretation, moreover, was grafted on to the Jewish interpretation, as is shown by this passage from the *Shepherd* of Hermas: "The great tree which spreads its shadow over the plains and the mountains and over the whole earth is the Law of God, given to the whole world. And this Law is the Son of God, preached unto the farthest ends of the earth. The peoples under its shadow are those who have heard the preaching and have believed in Him".[84]

Hermas does not explicitly mention the Cross. But for every Christian it was by His redemptive act, by His saving death, that the Son of God brought life to men; it was therefore essentially on the Cross that Christ was a "Tree of Life". And so it is only natural that the first great theologian of the Redemption, Origen, should be the one to insist most on the Christological interpretation of the passage in Proverbs. Here, from amongst other passages, is one taken from his treatise on Prayer:

The supersubstantial bread, which is the Logos of God, seems to me to be called in the Scriptures by another name, that of the Tree of Life, thanks to which he who stretches out his hand to take of it will live for ever (Gen. ii. 9); and by a third name, for it is called the Wisdom of God by Solomon, who says: "It is a Tree of Life to all who share in it, assured to those who go towards it as towards the Lord".[85]

This of course is simply one particular example of that identification between Christ and Wisdom which is itself only one aspect of the relationship established from the very beginning of Christianity between the Old and New Testaments.

Another passage from the Old Testament deserves to be quoted here, though it has attracted less attention from Christian writers. It is an account of a dream by Nabuchodonosor and is to be found in the Book of Daniel:

I saw, and behold a tree in the midst of the earth and the height thereof was exceeding great . . . the height thereof reached unto heaven; the sight thereof was even to the ends of all the earth. Its leaves were most beautiful, and its fruits exceeding much, and in it was food for all . . . And behold a watcher and a holy one came down from heaven. He cried aloud . . .: Cut down the tree and chop off the branches . . . leave the stump of its roots in the earth, and let it be tied with a band of iron and of brass . . . Let his heart be changed from man's, and let a beast's heart be given him . . .[86]

Here then is a tree which, one suddenly realises, is a human being whose heart is being torn out. "Sudden changes in the recording of the images are characteristic of the apocalyptic style."[87] This, no doubt, is simply a bold comparison of a kind natural enough in a dream—and in any case, as is immediately explained by Daniel when he is called into consultation, the being in question is the wicked king Nabuchodonosor.

It could hardly occur to any Christian reader, therefore, to apply this passage directly to the -crucified Saviour, but it nevertheless remains a fact that this passage provides us with yet another piece of evidence from pre-Christian times of the kind of imagery that was one day to impose itself on the author of our Paschal Homily.

Even now, however, from both the Christian and the Buddhist points of view, our question has only been pushed back a stage further; moreover, the commentary on the passage in Proverbs ignores the third term of our original equation—the Pillar. Let us say, then, more generally, that the ideas that existed in India before Buddhism, and which are sufficient to explain the pillar at Sanchi, are themselves derived from a source of myths which was not peculiar to India. The Tree of Life, the Axis of the world, the Pillar supporting the sun, the Cosmic Giant, are all to be found in Persia as well as India; they are Semitic as well as Indo-European—not to speak of the Far East. They are found in fact everywhere. Assyrian art, for example, contains many representations of the Tree of Life. According to the Babylonian tradition a tree whose fruit is precious stones is set up in the garden of the gods at Eridu. The epic of Gilgamesh mentions this, and Ezechiel alludes to it in his prophecy against the king of Tyre:

> Thou wast in the pleasure of the paradise of God,
> And every precious stone was thy covering . . .
> I set thee in the holy mountain of God,
> Thou hast walked in the midst of the stones of fire[88]

and again in his description of the new Holy Land, which was later to inspire the Apocalypse.[89] In Egypt, on a low relief at Abousir dating from the time of the nineteenth dynasty, "a goddess of whom only the arm is visible is seen rising from the stem of a date-palm; in one hand she bears a table of offerings and in the other a libation bowl"; on a coffin of the twenty-first dynasty which has been preserved in the museum at

Cairo, a goddess rises in the same way from the trunk of a sycamore-tree.[90] The famous Indian Pillar at Sarnath, which has often been looked upon—wrongly, as we have shown—as a Buddhist monument, but which is certainly a cosmic pillar, possesses certain characteristics that suggest a Babylonian (and Egyptian) influence, passed on by the art of the Achemenides.[91] Mesopotamia had symbols made up of a solar disc placed on top of a stem or pole.[92] The image of the great goddess, which seems at one time to have been venerated throughout the East, was associated with the image of a tree or a gigantic pillar, symbolising the tree on the mountain supporting the vault of heaven; "a kind of house of waters whence descend the rivers in all four directions".[93] Jean Przyluski found the same thing represented in a "many-branched tree on the seal belonging to Mohenjo-Daro" and in a "stylised column on the goblet of Goulea".[94] The Indian tree asvattha has been compared with the Atlas of our own mythology.[95] The Yggdrasil of Scandinavia is also a cosmic tree embracing the three worlds; as is the Saxon Irminsul, described by Rodolf of Fulda as *universalis columna quasi sustinens omnia* (a cosmic pillar supporting all things). The Altaics believe that a giant pine-tree rises from the centre of the earth into the heavenly regions of Bai-Ulgan: this "column of the world", with its seven branches, being represented by their pole with its seven notches. The Buriats erect inside their tents a pole which comes out at the top, and the neophyte who climbs to the top of it is thus raised to heaven.[96] The capital city of the perfect Chinese sovereign is to be found at the centre of the universe, near to the miraculous tree, "the wood", set up at the point of intersection of the three cosmic zones, heaven, earth, hell.[97] Finally, all over Europe and Asia there are myths explaining the formation of the world as the dismembering of a giant or god or primordial man. These symbols, or others of a similar kind—all of which were originally connected with sacrificial rites—are mixed up in a variety of combinations; but because of the idea which they contain, more or less explicitly, of a

sacred centre to the universe, they can all be said to be closely
allied to each other—or, rather, each one simply explains in its
own way the same total conception, which was in existence, in
a confused state at least, antecedently to it. That is why, even
when, for example, only the Tree is mentioned, it contains the
full symbolic force of the Pillar, the Axis of the world;[98] it
expresses, by itself alone, all the immanent energy of the.
cosmos.[99]

Here, then, we have two manifestations, two utilisations
of an ancient universal myth by two great historical religions.
In this particular case neither the Buddhist nor the Christian
imagination had anything to invent: both found ready to hand,
combined in one way or another, all the elements from which
they were to draw their own particular symbol.[100] Must one
therefore believe that these two great religions did no more than
gather the old mythological speculations to their bosoms and
give them new life? To this conclusion at least tend the
observations of A. K. Coomaraswamy. Writing from a point of
view which rather recalls that adopted by Emile Sénart in his
well-known essay on the Buddha, he says: "The fact that the
ancient symbol of the Tree of Life found in the Vedas and
Upanishads should have been chosen to represent the Buddha,
is highly significant; for . . . every traditional symbol carries
with it its original value even when it is used or is intended to
be used in a restricted sense. To appreciate to the full the
contents of Buddhist symbolism, it is necessary to study the
fundamental implications of the symbols employed by Buddhism. Only a knowledge of these symbols in their total significance can enlighten us as to their value when they are used in
a fully developed Buddhology."[101] From the purely metho-
dological point of view these remarks are perfectly true. But
they seem to have taken on a far wider significance in the mind
of their author; for a little further on we come across a statement of what is nothing less than a pure syncretism: ". . . Agni,
Vaisvanara, Christ, the idea of Mahomet and others, are all,

ontologically, one. The historic account of the life of Buddha, for example, like that of the life of Christ, must be looked upon as a reflection or condensation of cosmic relationships. The Buddha Gautama is an incarnation of Agni."[102]

So far as Christianity is concerned, such a point of view is entirely false, as we shall see in a moment. As regards Buddhism, it is at least highly exaggerated. True though it may be that Indian thought as a whole shows a remarkable continuity "in its literary tradition as well as its plastic arts", and that Sakyamuni's disciples could embark upon the way he opened to them without experiencing any sense of breaking with all their old ways of thinking and feeling, whether popular or learned, it must nevertheless be recognised that, as Odette Viennot says, this continuity "is possibly more formal than real".[103] There can be no doubt that on both sides there was a more or less conscious utilisation of mythical facts that dated from considerably earlier.[104] But this utilisation is, after all, no more than a matter of language. However new or original or revolutionary or even transcendent a religion may be, when it endeavours to express itself it is obliged to borrow its language from the accumulated stock of centuries which it finds in the human environment in which it comes to birth and develops.[105] What must be considered, when it uses these images or myths or concepts for its own purposes, are the new objects to which it devotes them, the extent to which it re-groups and transforms them, and the degree of intensity with which it stamps upon them its own mark and spirit.

Now in the particular Christian case with which we are concerned there is no mistaking what happened. Into the old bottles new wine is poured, and it bursts them. The immediate context of the homily of the pseudo-Chrysostom shows convincingly, without prejudice to its very Pauline cosmic realism,[106] the kind of spiritual transposition which has been effected. The whole passage, which is very beautiful, should be read; here we must content ourselves with a few lines: "The Beginning, Middle and End, containing, encompassing and gathering all things unto Himself in indissoluble bonds, [He] became the true Mediator between God and man ... alongside Him two thieves were hanged, signifying the two peoples, the two thoughts of the soul ... We beg Thee, Lord God, Christ our eternal spiritual King, spread Thy mighty hands over Thy Church and over Thy people for ever Thine!"[107] Thus the universe is here the Church. The Church is the new macrocosm of which the Christian soul is a copy in miniature. The bonds of connection and "sympathy" upon which the ancient magic had been based here become in Christ (if one may thus express it) bonds of spiritual magic. The "people" and the "soul" reply to each other and influence each other reciprocally. Under the shadow of the dogma of the Redemption, the dogmas of the Mystical Body and the Communion of Saints rise into the apotheosis of the universal Christ.[108]

Notice finally that a similar utilisation of the same mythical material by two different religions does not necessarily mean the slightest fundamental similarity of doctrine or spirit between the two. Here, in both cases, the Founder is magnified. But even in the analogy itself a contrast appears. In Buddhism when the ancient myth is readopted the originality of the new faith becomes blurred and its spirituality begins to take on its old naturalistic hues. In Christianity, "all things are made new", and any attempt at a naturalistic explanation of it would be utterly against its nature. In Buddhism, the tree under which the Buddha's throne is placed ends by lording it over the person meditating in its shade:[109] this is already suggested in the legendary accounts of Sakyamuni's illumination and his fight with Mara, for though the Buddha is "the Awakened One", the Tree is "the great Awakener"; though the Buddha announces the Dharma, the Tree is the Axis, the Dharma itself in its eternal fixity. In Christianity the whole value of the Cross comes from the divine fruit hanging on its branches. In Buddhism, the tree of salvation is the tree of knowledge, acquired by man himself by means of mental concentration, and which of itself, by removing his thirst for being, dries up the source of becoming: its fruit is a jewel, brilliant but sterile; so true is this that though we have gone on calling it a "Tree of Life" because of its similarity to the others, in the end this begins to seem rather inappropriate.[110] In Christianity, it is the sap of the Tree which enables man to share in the "Living God"; it is the Tree which procures eternal life, the Tree of fruitful suffering, the Tree of hope, at whose foot the springs of life gush forth, the rivers of paradise, the sacraments of the Church. In Buddhism, the "unique fig-tree" is still a tree, one of an infinite number like itself, and the centre of a universe lost in time and space in an infinity of universes whose centre is nowhere. In Christianity, the Tree of the Cross is unique, it is the one Tree of light, bearing the one "True Sun". It alone deserves to be called unique—*super omnia ligna cedrorum tu sola excelsior*—because it alone bears, uniquely and finally, the Salvation of the world:

> *Ecce lignum crucis*
> *In quo salus mundi pependit.*

In Buddhism the cosmic Buddha who is identical with the Dharma is the impersonal void of Being, the essential Buddhahood into which Sakyamuni is absorbed by identifying himself with all the other Buddhas who have disappeared.[111] In Christianity the cosmic—or rather hyper-cosmic—Christ is still the person Jesus of Nazareth, Man and God to all eternity, the one author of salvation.

Finally, in Buddhism the centre of the world, the place where the support of the universe rests, is Buddha Gaya, i.e. the place of enlightenment. In Christianity this centre, which is not so much a point in space, a topographical height at the centre of the material universe, as an event in time, the culminating point of human history—is Calvary, where all things were obediently resigned into the hands of the Father; a place of sacrifice and great "cosmic combat",[112] over which rises the Cross.

A NOTE ON THE COMPARATIVE SYMBOLISM OF BUDDHIST AND CHRISTIAN PRIMITIVE ART

The identification of the Buddha with the Pillar-Tree, like the identification of Christ with the Cross, can be explained, as we have seen, by reasons drawn from the order of cosmic mysticism, but it may also have been facilitated by the symbolism which was essential to the primitive art of the two religions because in it there was never any attempt at a direct portrayal of Sakyamuni or Jesus.

In Buddhism this is a well-known and important fact: primitive Buddhist art is aniconic. "The fact has been repeated so often that it has become a commonplace: never—neither at Bharhut nor at Sanchi, not even where there is an inscription to tell us, if we could possibly be in any doubt about it, that here the Master is present—never is there any portrayal of the Buddha: an empty throne, an umbrella, a wheel, a trisula, footprints—these are all we ever see. Let it be added that this omission is made on purpose: the artistry with which the other characters are presented is quite sufficient to prove that if the Buddha is not portrayed where his presence seems to be most called for by the subject, this is because there was never any intention of portraying him".[1]

The main symbols of this iconography will be familiar: the birth of the Buddha is represented by a lotus, his enlightenment by the fig-tree at Buddha Gaya (with, occasionally, under the tree, a throne), his first sermon by a wheel (with or without an umbrella), often with a gazelle on either side (the Sermon of Benares was preached in the "gazelle park"), and his death by a stupa.[2] A riderless horse under an umbrella symbolises the vocation of the Bodhisattva; the paving-stone—which is to be seen twice, for example, on the eastern door at Sanchi— is the Buddha's covered walk, and stands for his actual presence.[3]

Many historians have connected this absence of any representations of the Buddha with the doctrine of nirvana: how is it possible to depict one who has "departed", the "dead god" (Oldenberg), a being who has vanished into space? But if this explanation were entirely correct there would be no portrayal of the Buddha even in his earlier lives, or else he would be portrayed in his final existence right up to the moment of Bodhi. Now, "the disciples who performed the 'pradaksina', i.e. went in a clockwise direction round the foot of the highly decorated stupas in Central India, would see a long series of low reliefs all dedicated to the glorification of the Buddha, who appears hundreds of times in a great variety of manifestations, all his previous lives being linked together in a long chain. But as soon as the ultimate aim of his long career is attained, at the moment of his final birth, he vanishes, and there is nothing left to see but the empty place which he should have occupied, or some material object symbolising his presence".[4] Thus narrowed down, this is the fact that remains to be explained; and two kinds of explanation exist—one as represented by Alfred Foucher, the other by Paul Mus.[5]

The last complete account which Foucher gave of his theory is contained in his *Etudes sur l'Art bouddhique de l'Inde*—"Evolution de l'art bouddhique, esquisse iconographique" (Tokyo, Maison franco-japonaise, 1928, pp. 7–50). According to this, the whole phenomenon can be explained as the result of the play of external circumstances. Having stated "the paradox behind this decorative art, which has as almost its sole aim the depiction of the legends, but which obstinately refuses to portray the figure of the Blessed One himself" (p. 10), Foucher attempts to find the reason of this "in the embryology of Buddhist art" (p. 46).

From the very beginning (in the fifth century B.C.), pilgrims coming to worship at the four holy places had bought little souvenirs, which depicted the holy places in a simple stylised way: these were the first humble productions of Buddhist art, "rudimentary representations", of a "childish simplicity", "hieroglyphics rather than pictures" (p. 15). By a natural association, these mementoes came to be looked upon as symbolic of the four incidents which had taken place there. With the passage of time the custom was erected into a law, as always happens in India: it was agreed that in the portrayal of any scene from the Master's life his presence could be evoked by one of these "emblems". This is why the Buddha's throne, for example, always remains empty on all the low reliefs of the old school. The sculptures may become more and more complicated or refined, their subjects more and more varied: the paradoxical void remains. Thus, "in its later development the old school always felt the influence of the admixture of religion and industry which it underwent at the very beginning at the hands of these makers of pious objects dwelling in the holy places. It was to this false start that it owed the fact of being forbidden by custom . . . to portray the essential character who should have figured at the centre of all its compositions" (pp. 37–38). But though the artists were for a long time unable to shake off the yoke of custom, by their astuteness they managed to circumvent it. There is nothing astonishing in the extraordinary development they gave to the double cycle of the *Jatakas* and the *Asokavadana*, i.e. incidents from the earlier lives of Sakyamuni and incidents that followed upon his death: "here they were not handicapped by any precedent"; they could portray the Bodhisattva or his disciples just as they liked. This double series of pictures was a "double derivative" for them (pp. 26 and 48)—like two vigorous shoots of a tree, whose main branch, "that of the life of the Buddha, always remains abnormal and, so to speak, stunted".

Such, then, is the mechanism by which the wheel, for example, first signified a place, Benares; then a scene, the first sermon; then in the middle of this scene (which it henceforth symbolised) a person, the Buddha; then, if need be, the same person in some other scene. A technical difficulty, added to the force of routine, helped to prevent any further development: how could one possibly have dared to invent a portrayal of the Buddha, above all things, when artistic tradition said nothing about him? And so, in the end, it was from the outside that this development came. "Unlikely as it may seem, it was finally reserved to Indo-Greek artists to create the artistic prototype of the Buddha" (p. 38).

"You see," Foucher concludes, "how clear and coherent everything becomes" (p. 18). Perhaps even a little too clear—perhaps with a little too much of the kind of coherence and clarity upon which Voltaire for instance flattered himself. Foucher aimed "to set aside all theories and give a faithful account of the facts" (p. 7). There is indeed no one who is better acquainted with the facts than he, and no one who has done more to pass the facts on to us; it is true, also, that with his profound knowledge of Indian Buddhist art he managed to throw new light upon the Sakyamuni legend.[6] The reconstitution which he has attempted to make raises a number of difficulties, for all that. His conclusion has been questioned by more than one historian: it does not seem to be absolutely certain that the first human representation of the Buddha comes from the Indo-Greek school, nor that all the others derive from it.[7] But the point from which he starts seems more debatable still. Buddhist art is supposed to have taken its rise "from the little material souvenirs that were sold to pilgrims in the fifth century B.C. by the makers of pious objects who dwelt in the four holy places" (p. 13). But is it likely that such a stream of pilgrims, and such intense commercial activity, should have sprung up so soon? The "little lumps of clay with a stamp on them that were obviously within the range of everyone's pocket, and which were to be found more or less everywhere, from Afghànistan to Annam" appeared at a later date. Foucher makes a comparison with the metal *signacula* used by Christian pilgrims in the Middle Ages; but can the sale of such objects be imagined at Jerusalem during the first centuries of Christianity, before there was any Christian art? He also mentions the square pieces of Indian money, some of which date back as far as the fourth century B.C. and bear

Buddhist symbols (pp. 12-15); but who is to prove that these pieces of money correspond to the *signacula* sold to Christian pilgrims? And, in any case, in the aniconic art of early Buddhism there are sculptures—such as our "cosmic tree" and the like—which it is absolutely impossible to describe as examples of a rudimentary or popular or commercial kind of art. [8]

The first stage in the process described by Foucher, the change from a stylised representation of a place to the symbolic representation of the incident which occurred at that place, can easily be imagined. The stupa at Kusinagara evokes the scene at which nirvana was achieved, the tree at Buddha-Gaya the moment of Enlightenment (though there is a considerable difference between a tree and an empty throne under a tree). But it is considerably more difficult to imagine how, after the incident has come to be depicted, the original symbol (especially when this happens to be a void, a total absence) comes to stand for the principal character. [9] The paradox becomes more bewildering still when the same symbol is used in a totally different scene. And it hardly seems possible to invoke the force of custom, when the whole point is that there are so many innovations to be taken into account.

Foucher, it is true, makes a great deal of a certain technical difficulty. Since from the very beginning there had never been any attempt at a portrayal of the Buddha as a person, as time went on the artists were bound to feel less and less able to manufacture his portrait, especially when they were so strictly bound by the rules of their art. But why should the young Siddharta have been more difficult to portray than all the other characters, whose actual appearance was equally unknown? As for the type of the perfect Buddha, though there was no artistic tradition about him there was certainly a very precise and detailed literary tradition, so that as soon as he began to be portrayed his type was fixed at once. "Ancient India . . . had two long lists of the external characteristics attributed to the individual known as the Buddha, the thirty-two signs of the Great Man (Mahapurusa) and the eighty secondary marks;

so that when the sculptors of Gandara got to work on their effigies of the Buddha, they simply had to follow rules that already existed."[10]

Paul Mus has therefore suggested another explanation: from the moment of his final birth the Buddha was a transcendent being, transported into regions beyond this world of becoming. "Though effigies sufficed for the supernumeraries, or to illustrate the Buddha's earlier lives, they were no longer suitable for him when he had been proclaimed in the texts as being, at the moment of his final birth, the Ancient of the World, the highest of all beings. If this supposition is true, the Buddha is absent, not because the attempt to portray him directly was renounced, but because an attempt was made to discover a kind of representation that was superior to direct portrayal."[11] His evocation by way of symbols is not therefore a makeshift, but a kind of art which from the religious point of view is superior to a direct representation of the human figure. Perhaps the primitive faith needed to lose some of its early vigour before it could be reduced to the latter.[12]

The first advantage of this is that it does away with the improbabilities involved in the first explanation and also seems to achieve a greater degree of depth: it sees more in the aniconism of primitive Buddhist art than a simple "anomaly". It also accounts, by analogy, for another peculiarity which had in fact been pointed out by Foucher himself; for not only had the artists "done their best to illustrate the Buddha's career in detail without portraying the Buddha himself", but, "as though this major difficulty was not enough, they had imposed a further restriction upon themselves . . .", making it a law "not to portray anyone except laymen amongst the disciples, and from amongst the religious themselves, only heretics before their conversion. Thus they deliberately endeavoured to show us the Master's work—which consisted essentially in the foundation of a monastic order—not only without letting us see the founder, but even without showing us a single monk".[13]

Nevertheless, if the aniconism of early Buddhist art is thus sufficiently explained, the nature of the symbolism which went with it is still not quite clear. It is true that the idea of a purely accidental and conventional symbolism, such as would result from Foucher's theory, has been avoided. We know henceforth that the first Buddhist sculptors were guided by "metaphysical" intentions (less consciously, perhaps, and less explicitly than readers of Paul Mus might be tempted to think on reading his extremely lucid analysis of these things); but it still seems necessary to go into a little more detail.

The symbolism does not appear to have been based on purely negative considerations, for there are a number of positive symbols which seem to have been very aptly chosen to suggest the idea of the Buddha's transcendence—the cankrama, for instance. It is known that when the Buddha was born, he did not touch the ground with his feet. Now he "preserved this privilege all his life: his feet were never soiled by contact with any dust or mud, but their soles always lay absolutely flat on the ground, however uneven it might be. Burnouf has already shown that this sign of the great man signifies the levelling of the ground under his feet: stones and paths vanish, and the earth itself, with its valleys filled in and its mountains laid low, becomes a stretch of ground as flat as a lake. There could hardly be a better way of suggesting the transcendent height from which the Master looks down upon us. In short, when the later iconography represents Sakyamuni as standing or sitting upon a lotus raised above the ground, which is crowded with his worshippers, it is only adopting the same kind of symbolism as that which inspired the old sculptors".[14]

But, Paul Mus adds, this symbolism was not merely doctrinal. There was a magical intention behind it too. The symbols did not only signify the Buddha's transcendence, they were concrete helps to raise his followers into that indescribable condition of being in which they could communicate with the transcendent object of their religion. They were "instruments of magic to draw us towards the personality of the Buddha, who was thus by this artifice transferred into conditions of existence different from our own".[15] Mus supports his argument by facts drawn from pre-Buddhist India and the aniconic cult of local spirits, which often coincides with that of the holy places of Buddhism.[16] It would take too long to go into the subject here; all that need be said is that the religious symbolism never seems in concrete fact to be purely intellectual in nature.

There remains a final point, which brings us to the very heart of our subject. The symbols used in the aniconic art of primitive Buddhism did not simply take the place of the Master; they were the image of his person. The mythological significance was applied directly from the Tree, the Pillar, the Lotus, to the Buddha himself, so that there was, if not an absolute identification, at least an intrinsic connection between the Buddha and the object by which he was symbolised. This theory, which has won the support of Paul Mus, is maintained by Ananda K. Coomaraswamy in his study of the pillar at Sanchi, where, as we have seen, the representation of a real person can be discerned through the symbolism. The same is true of the Throne, whose symbolism has recently been explained by Mlle. Auboyer as absolutely identical with that of the Tree and the Pillar.[17] The symbols "do not take the place of the Buddha, they are the Buddha".[18]

It would be highly misleading to speak of any aniconic Christian art; all that can be said is that in its early stages Christian art was eminently symbolic. If the direct portrayal of Christ appears comparatively late, this is for different reasons from those which prevented any portrayal of the Buddha. Not only is all religious art naturally symbolic, but the Christians had inherited from the Jews a horror of the worship of images,[19] and were obliged to guard against idolatry very carefully[20]—though this did not prevent them from allowing larger scope than was customary amongst the Jews to the production of paintings and sculptures of actual people as a means of artistic decoration and teaching. Perhaps in certain cases reasons of prudence prevented any direct portrayal, because of the danger of persecution. The appearance of the crucifix was no doubt delayed because of the horror with which the cross was looked upon by pagans and even by the Christians themselves: it represented a kind of punishment that was not only cruel but humiliating—punishment to which slaves were subject, a target for mockery. Perhaps a "feeling of awe"[21] entered into the matter too. Finally, the Christians who were instructed by St. Paul would have said with him: "I no longer wish to know Christ according to the flesh"; they did not have the same sort of religious curiosity about the episodes—even the essential episodes—in the earthly life of Christ as later Christians were to have, and so they were less concerned with portraying them. But when they did come to do this the figure of Christ was treated in exactly the same way as the figures of all the other characters.

The first pictures of Christ were apparently venerated by heretics and were of pagan origin; they later filtered through into a few orthodox Christian circles composed of converts from paganism. Eusebius only half approves of them: he prevailed upon the Empress Constantia not to have one painted. Epiphanus, more radical, prided himself on having pulled down a veil hanging at the door of a church in Palestine on which there was a painting of Christ. Such facts are well known. In the Church as a whole the first "Christs" are symbols of Christ inspired either by the imagery of the Gospels or by figures of pagan art, or by both at once: there is the Lamb carrying its cross, or lying at the foot of a cross, or with a cross on its forehead;[22] there is the Good Shepherd, or Orpheus, and the Good Shepherd has the same features as the herdsman, Hermes. On a sarcophagus dating from the fourth century discovered recently during the excavations at St. Peter's, there is a frieze which portrays by means of symbols a number of episodes in the life of Our Lord: one lamb is baptising another, and above the latter a dove can be seen. There is another kind of symbolism which consists in using scenes from the Old Testament to signify scenes from the Gospels or the Christian life: the sacrifice of Abraham or Melchisedech, Jonas being spewed out by the whale, Noe, Moses, etc. A splendid general effect is given by a mural painting in the cemetery at Calliste: on the left is an altar (the priest being on the left of the altar, the Church on the right); on the right, Abraham about to sacrifice his son; in the middle, a mystic feast, consisting of seven guests each with a basket in front of him—reminding one of the multiplication of the loaves (though this central scene is not directly related to the Last Supper any more than the sacrifice of Isaac refers to Calvary). When a rather more concentrated style is adopted the same person can be at the same time Moses and St. Peter, according to the emblems he carries in each of his hands. Thus in its figurative imagery as in its teaching, the New Testament used the Old as its intermediary, and there is no need to deduce from this any kind of objection on principle to the representation of Christ. At a later date scenes from the Gospels suggested by scenes from the Old Testament are also portrayed opposite each other.

It is in the third century that there appears what is probably an image of Christ during His Passion, possibly from the scene of the Scourging, at the cemetery in Praetextatus. Other images follow—on sarcophagi, in mosaics (for instance, the great mosaic at St. Pudentiana) and in scenes from the Gospels, which, from the beginning of the sixth century, become, in the east, at least, more realistic in treatment. The cross appears later (the one at St. Pudentiana has already been mentioned). The "Latin cross", which was recently discovered at Herculaneum, and said to date from the second century, is certainly not a Christian symbol. Very few crosses have been found on Christian epitaphs before the time of Constantine, and most of these remain doubtful or must be rejected as spurious. Many are anchors in the shape of a cross rather than actual crosses. The reason is that to begin with the cross itself, like Christ, was symbolised rather than represented, symbolised on quite a large scale and by a variety of things, either natural or manufactured. The *Epistle of Barnabas* provides us with "the first known reference to the importance of the cross as an emblem".[23] Clement of Alexandria[24] allowed Christians to have symbols of the cross engraved on their rings—for instance, an anchor, or a ship sailing in the wind. The anchor, which was used in the first place merely as a symbol of peace[25] and hope, seems to have been the first of these symbols. The sign of the cross—apparently, like so much else, of Gnostic origin— is mentioned by Tertullian[26] and St. Cyprian[27] as having been used by orthodox Christians in the third century. But as a general rule there is "no cross, no monogram of the name Jesus, no representation of the Passion" before the fourth century. Then, towards the end of his reign, Constantine passed a law which abolished the penalty of crucifixion. "Although Eusebius does not mention this", says Sulzberger, "there is no doubt about it, and it is a very important fact in the history of the cross"; "when even the memory of crucifixion had almost disappeared, there were no further qualms about portraying the cross without any disguises".[28] This was becoming quite common at about the beginning of the fifth century.

CHAPTER III

DIFFERENT MANIFESTATIONS OF CHRIST AND THE BUDDHA

Two great religious systems, however different they may be from each other, are bound to offer a great many points of comparison, and so it is not surprising that historians should have found a number of passages in Christian writings which can be compared with passages in Buddhist writings, especially as more and more of these have come to be known. The comparisons that have been made are sometimes quite startling, and they seem to make it necessary to assume some kind of real connection between the two; at other times they are, to say the least, highly ingenious; usually, however, it must be confessed, they seem superficial, vague, arbitrary and even fantastic, especially as regards the far-fetched conclusions that are drawn from them. To avoid this kind of error, this chapter will remain within rigidly circumscribed limits. I simply wish to draw attention to a few passages from Christian writings, for the most part Alexandrian in origin, which seem to suggest a certain analogy with a number of Buddhist passages concerning the doctrine of the Trikaya or its antecedents.

The resemblances will, I believe, appear of their own accord. The question that arises is whether we have to assume some kind of historical connection, established by some means or other, between the ideas stated or suggested in the two kinds of passages: is everything to be put down to the activity of the human mind, manifesting itself, now here, now there, in a series of similar processes? In the present state of our knowledge, not only of Buddhist literature, but of the history of the relationship between India and the Mediterranean,[1] it would be presumptuous to attempt to answer this question here. If any influence is to be admitted, there is still the question of which way it worked. There are quite a number of important points on which the presumption today would be in favour of the West as the prior agent—a West which, it is true, begins at Persia. According to some recent historians there are "Gnostic" influences in the Prajnaparamita and neo-Platonic echoes in the philosophy of Asanga, introduced into India by the Mithraic mysteries of Hellenistic cosmology, and these signs oblige us to recognise a Western influence on the development of Buddhism.[2] There are difficulties in the way of accepting this point of view, however, and these signs would be more convincing if the dates were not usually so uncertain.[3] At the same time, the suggestion of an alternative influence at a slightly earlier period is not to be dismissed; and it is possible that on certain points the influence was reciprocal. The general question of an Indian influence on the formation of neo-Platonism remains undecided.[4] The existence of a Buddhist colony in the great city of Alexandria has not yet been finally disproved, and it seems that the Alexandrians were at least slightly better acquainted with Buddhist affairs than the inhabitants of most of the other parts of the Empire.[5] After the discovery of the monsoon in A.D. 47 more regular contact was made possible between the great port and the coasts of India. Borrowings from Buddhism have frequently been pointed out, often with a high degree of probability, in several of the apocryphal writings of Christianity, in Jewish Christian literature, and in the Gnostics, particularly Basilides, etc.

Whatever truth there may be in these theories, we nevertheless recognise, with de la Vallée-Poussin and Paul Mus, that the Mahayana is written in the *koiné* of India and not in that of the Mediterranean basin, though we should not be so certain about the alternative assertion at least as regards what is usually described as Alexandrian Gnosticism. However this may be, the texts from which we shall quote seem to us worth consideration. The record which has been amassed so patiently by our Buddhist historians with the aim of discovering a Western element in the thought of the Great Vehicle, or conversely a Buddhist element in Gnosticism, is, after all, not so bulky that one can afford to neglect any information, however minute, which might eventually help to swell it.[6] And apart from the problem of influences, we may find matter for reflection and instruction in the comparison of these passages.

I

A man to men
and an angel to the angels.

(i) The Buddha and the Eight Classes of Beings

The *Mahaparinibbana-sutta*, a work of the Pali Canon, contains a passage in which Paul Mus, following de la Vallée-Poussin, sees—along with the mysterious passages on "the body of the law" and "the heritage of the law"—one of the earliest infiltrations of the Great Vehicle into this Canon.[7] It occurs in the third chapter, n. 21–23, and is a pronouncement by the Buddha about himself, addressed to Ananda:

O Ananda, there are eight kinds of "assemblies". What are they? They are the assemblies of the nobles, the brahmans, the ordinary people, the ascetics, the gods who are the companions of the four guardians of the world, the gods of the world of Mara, the gods of the heaven of Brahma. Before entering the assembly of the nobles and engaging in conversation with them, I make myself look like them and I make my voice like theirs. Then by speaking about religion to them I teach them, enlighten them, animate them, and fill them with joy. But they do not recognise me whilst I am speaking to them. "Who," they think to themselves, "is this being who is teaching us, a god or a man?" And when I disappear, after having taught them, enlightened them, animated them and filled them with joy, they still do not know who I am: "Who", they ask, "is this person who has disappeared, a god or a man?"[8]

(ii) The Logos and the Angels according to Origen

Now in his commentary on the Gospel according to St. John, Origen speaks in an almost identical way. He applies to the Logos, but with a totally different meaning, the words of St. Paul when he says of himself that he makes himself all things to all men: "Therefore the Saviour, in a far more divine manner than Paul, made Himself all things to all men in order to save or perfect all living beings. And undoubtedly he made himself a man to men and an angel to the angels: καὶ σαφῶς γέγονεν ἀνθρώποις ἄνθρωπος καὶ ἀγγέλοις ἄγγελος. And if none of the faithful doubts that He became man, let us be equally certain that He became an angel, in view of the appearances of angels, and the words spoken by angels, in the Scriptures."[9]

De la Vallée-Poussin has already pointed out the connection between this passage from Origen and Buddhist teaching in a note to his appendix to the *Siddhis* of Huian Tsang.[10] It is true that there are a number of commentators on Origen who consider this connection entirely imaginary: Huet, followed by Prat, tries to minimise the significance of Origen's words and side-tracks the discussion onto the problem of the theophanies in the Old Testament.[11] However, in this passage at least Origen makes no mention of the theophanies, except incidentally: according to him it is definitely "for the angels"— and therefore "amongst the angels"—that the Saviour "became an angel" and not, in the first place, in order to speak to men about God. His appearances in angelic form to men are simply a further proof of this—as what follows in the text shows clearly.[12] If the Saviour, according to the Apocalypse, is the Beginning and End, i.e. God and Man, He is likewise "all that comes in between"; if He is given these two names, "it is so that it will be quite clear that he Has assumed all things unto Himself".

In any case, this is not the only passage of the kind in Origen's writings. Its meaning will become clearer when seen in the light of a passage from the *Eighth Homily on Genesis*, in which these very theophanies give him the opportunity to reveal the relationship between the Saviour and the angels: "It is an angel who is said here to have spoken to Abraham, and it subsequently becomes clear that this angel is the Lord; whence I conclude that just as 'He was recognised as a man by His appearance' when He appeared amongst men, in the same way when He appeared amongst the angels He was recognised as an angel by His appearance."[13]

There is a similar argument in the *Commentary on the Epistle to the Romans*:

He, the Word made flesh, appeared to those who are in the flesh . . .; when He appeared to the angels, He did not appear without the Gospel, any more than He did to us men . . . If therefore, when He appeared to us men, He did not appear without the Gospel, it seems that as a consequence one must say that to the angelic order too He did not appear without the Gospel. Perhaps this is that Eternal Gospel which we recollect St. John to have spoken of to us. And if, moreover, there is reason for thinking that He behaved similarly towards the other heavenly orders, appearing to each of them in their own particular form and proclaiming peace to them. . . .[14]

Other passages, it is true, are not quite as clear as this. Some simply enunciate the general principle: "Is qui pro omnium salute FACTUS EST OMNIA."[15] Others, again, seem to envisage different states or different manifestations of the Logos directed entirely towards men, the Logos adapting Himself to their various conditions. Thus, in the *Commentary on St. Matthew*: "If you can contemplate the Logos restored to His original condition after becoming flesh and making Himself all things to all men, making Himself into whatever each particular person needed in order to win them all; if you can contemplate Him restored to the condition in which He becomes what He was at the beginning with God . . ."[16]

Lastly, there are some passages which seem at first sight to require a similar explanation to that given of the texts on St. John, Genesis and the Epistle to the Romans; but such an explanation does not always seem absolutely essential, and sometimes a quite different explanation is possible—is, indeed, demanded by the passage. This is the case, it seems to us, as regards this passage from the *First Homily on Leviticus*, n. 3: "There was a double sacrifice in this, which was in harmony with both earthly and heavenly things."[17] This can be explained, as Bigg[18] has explained it, by saying that the blood which flowed at the gates of Jerusalem was shed mystically on the Altar on high. Or there is this other passage from the *Commentary on St. John*, in which Origen says that Christ died, not only for men but for all who had sinned—for example, the heavenly bodies; but that this redemption of all things was perfectly accomplished by the single sacrifice on Calvary.[19] In these various passages, Origen, drawing his inspiration from the Epistle to the Hebrews, "speaks as a theologian rather than a historian";[20] his aim is to assert the universality of the Redemption, the unlimited efficacy of the blood shed upon the Cross.[21]

The three passages quoted earlier, however, are too precise in character to be susceptible of this kind of interpretation. The thought which they contain bears a strange resemblance to that of the *Parinibbana-sutta*.

(iii) *The Manifestations of God according to Philo*

This idea of Origen's seems to be a Christian adaptation of an Alexandrian idea very dear to Philo,[22] who frequently refers to appearances of the Divine which are graduated according to the nature of the beings to whom He wishes to appear. Thus, in these two passages from the *De somniis*:

It is natural that to the incorporeal souls who are His intimates God should manifest Himself as He is, behaving as a friend with friends; but that to those who are still in the body He should appear in the form of an angel; not that He changes His nature, which is immutable, but by putting a different image of Himself into the imagination in such a way that the image seems not to be imagined but the original form itself . . .

Why should we be surprised, then, if God appears in the form of an angel, and sometimes even appears to men in this form in order to help those who need Him? Thus, when it is said in Scripture: "I am the God who appeared to you in the form of God", realise that in His appearance He took on the form of an angel (without changing His nature) in order to help someone who could not have seen the true God in any other way. Just as those who cannot look at the sun itself can see its reflection, and see the haloes of the moon as the moon itself, so the image of God, His Logos, is perceived as God Himself.[23]

There is therefore no need to assume that Origen borrowed directly from any Buddhist source.

(iv) Similar Doctrines before Origen

Nor is it necessary to assume that Origen is here directly dependent upon Philo. This Buddhist and Alexandrian idea had in fact penetrated into certain Christian circles before his time. For example, there is in the first place *The Ascension of Isaias*, Chapters x and xi:[24]

[Ch. x] . . . And I heard the voice of the Highest . . . saying to my Lord the Christ . . .: "Arise and descend through all the heavens, then shalt Thou descend to the firmament and to this world . . . And Thou shalt be transformed into the form of the angels of the firmament and also into the form of the angels who are in Sheol."

. . . When He descended into the fifth heaven and was transformed . . . according to the appearance of the angels who were there, they did not worship Him because His appearance was like their own. Then He descended into the fourth heaven and was transformed into the appearance of the angels who were there; and when they saw Him, they did not worship Him . . . for His appearance was like unto their appearance. [And so for the third, second and first heavens.]

And again He descended into the firmament where lives the prince of this world, and He gave the password to those who were on the left, and His appearance was like unto theirs . . . And when He descended and made Himself like unto the angels of the air He was Himself like one of them . . .

[Ch. xi] And after that . . . I saw a woman of the family of the prophet David, whose name was Mary.

There is also the *Conversation of the Risen Jesus with His Disciples after the Resurrection*, a Gnostic work of the second century.[25] The Lord is speaking: "When I come down from the all-powerful Father, when I travel through the heavens . . . I am like unto the heavenly beings, the angels and archangels; when I travel through the heavens under their scrutiny I am like one of them . . . The archangels Michael, Gabriel, Uriel and Raphael followed Me to the borders of the fifth firmament because I resembled them."[26]

A little later the Lord adds: "Do you not remember that I once said to you that to the angels I seemed like an angel? . . . Then, in the likeness of the archangel Gabriel I Myself appeared to the Virgin Mary . . . I, the Word, entered into her . . . and thus I became My own minister . . ."[27] Here, strangely united, are the two ideas which we came across separately in Origen.[28]

The *Pistis Sophia* likewise causes the Saviour to say: "When

I set out and came down into this world, I passed through the Archons of the Sphere, I took on the appearance of the angel Gabriel so that the Archons of the Aeons should not recognise Me."[29]

The Gnosis of the Sethians (who are perhaps the Ophites) included a similar scheme, if we are to believe the summary of it given by St. Irenaeus in his *Adversus Haereses*, l. I, c. 30, n. 12: "They say that Christ descended through the seven heavens, looking like their son . . ."[30]

The same idea occurs again, according to St. Irenaeus, in Simon Magus—and no doubt it was attributed to the "father of all the heretics" because it was common amongst the "Gnostic" groups of the second century. Thus according to Irenaeus, Simon claimed that his spouse Helen was Ennoia, the first Thought, from whom all beings sprang: "He shows us this 'Ennoia' leaving him and descending into the lower regions, engendering the angels and the Powers by whom, he says, this world was made. But after she had brought them to birth, they kept her prisoner because they were jealous of her, and inflicted every kind of insult upon her, so that she should not return to her father—to such an extent that she even found herself confined in a human body."[31]

In this form the idea is connected with a kind of pessimism common enough in Gnostic systems of thought. The idea is that of a captivity by the angels, not a voluntary sojourn amongst them for the purpose of teaching them. The *Ascension of Isaias*, the *Conversation of the Risen Jesus*, the Sethian myth, simply speak of a passage through the regions of the heavenly Powers, a journey necessary topographically in order to enable the traveller to come down to earth. The *Pistis Sophia* states or emphasises the fact that it is a ruse adopted by the Saviour in an endeavour to pass incognito through the abodes of the Powers so that He shall not be detained there. All these texts provide variations on the well-known theme of a descent through the spheres. They are far less important from our point of view than the passages from Origen which we quoted earlier, for they show far less resemblance to our Buddhist passages. There is, however, another idea, which is very similar to ideas found in Origen and Buddhism, in the first Armenian fragment of Irenaeus:[32]

> The Law, the Prophets and the Gospels taught that Christ was born of a Virgin, suffered on the cross, was raised from the dead, and ascended into heaven, where He reigns in glory for ever. He is the true Thought, the Word of God whom they announced, who was born from the beginning and present at the creation of all things, who created man, in whom were all things: He was a patriarch amongst the patriarchs, a law amongst the laws, a high priest·amongst the priests, a supreme sovereign amongst the kings, a prophet amongst the prophets, an angel amongst the angels, a man amongst men, the Son of God, God of God, King for ever. He it was who watched over the Ark, who led Abraham, who bound himself to Isaac, who lived in a foreign land with Jacob, who was sold with Joseph, was given the Commandments with Moses, dictated the laws to the people, divided up the land with Joshua amongst the tribes, sang with David, revealed His sufferings to the Prophets, took flesh of the Virgin . . .
>
> He is the resurrection of the dead, the salvation of lost souls, the light to those who are in darkness, the means of salvation to those born outside the true way, the guide of those who have gone astray . . . the Bridegroom of the Church. God of God, Son of the Father, Jesus Christ the everlasting King. Amen.

This idea of an "angelisation" of the Word was sufficiently widespread for Tertullian to feel obliged to refute it in his *Liber de carne Christi*:[33]

> But, they say, Christ became an angel [*angelum gestavit*]. Why? For the same reason that He became man. It must

therefore have been from the same cause . . . This cause was the salvation of man—i.e. to restore that which had perished. Man had perished, it was necessary that man should be restored. But there was no reason for Christ to become an angel. For, although we know that some angels fell "into the fire prepared for the devil and his angels", they were never given any promise that they would be restored. Christ received from His Father no commandment concerning the salvation of the angels . . . Why then did He become an angel, unless it was to achieve the salvation of man by being a powerful guard over the body? . . . Could it be to free man by means of an angel?

(v) A comparison of these Buddhist and Christian Passages

Thus Jews and Christians, Gnostics and Orthodox, theologians like Irenaeus and thinkers like Origen, present us with similar passages whose wording is often identical. Whatever differences there may be in their moral significance or in the spirit informing them, all these passages have a common idea, the idea of an "economy" in the manifestations of the divine, an "economy" which the Buddhists applied to the manifestations of the Buddha. Christ is an angel amongst the angels as the Buddha is a Bodhisattva amongst the Bodhisattvas, a god amongst the gods.

For the rest, even when the wording is identical, the differences between the two naturally remain very great, governed as they are by their religious context as a whole. If, in particular, we compare Origen's ideas with those in the *Parinibbana-sutta*, one essential difference becomes clear. The accusations of a concealed Docetism which have been levelled against Origen are far from being justified. His affirmation of the Logos as "an angel amongst the angels" may seem to us strange, indeed phantasmagorical. It was condemned as scandalous after his death, in the fourth anathema pronounced by the Council of 543 against the Origenism of the Palestinian monks of the day:

Anathema on whoever says or holds that the Word of God assumed the appearance of all the heavenly orders, became a cherub amongst the cherubim, a seraph amongst the seraphim, in a word, one like unto all the Virtues on high. [34]

It was not, however, a way of refining the mystery of the Incarnation, any more than was the belief in the repeated interruptions of the course of sacred history by the Logos, a belief which is also found in the realistic Irenaeus. On the contrary, as may have been noticed, it is on the fact of the Incarnation that Origen begins by taking his stand: "If there is no believer who doubts that He became man . . ." [35] So far is it from the truth to say that the Incarnation is weakened, that in another place the earlier manifestations of the Logos in human history are imagined too directly as a coming in the flesh, and seem to a modern reader far too "substantial": "Substantialiter semper Christus praesens fuit et in Moyse et in Prophetis, magis autem in angelis ministrantibus saluti humanae." [36] Moreover, every time the opportunity presents itself Origen expresses in the strongest terms his faith in the reality of the Incarnation—as for instance in this fragment on the Epistle to the Galatians: "Adjungendum est etiam . . . quoniam corpus Christi non erat alienum a terrena substantia." [37]

There is even less need to insist on this in the case of Irenaeus, whose irreducible antagonism to the doctrine of Docetism is well known, as in the words: "Non enim aliud videbatur et aliud erat . . . sed quod erat, hoc et videbatur." [38] For the rest, the passage which we quoted from the first Armenian fragment stands at the beginning of a tradition in which there are to be found names like that of St. Augustine, [39] who has certainly never been suspected of any heretical opinions on this point.

In short, the human reality and, if one may say so, the bodily solidity which Origen and Irenaeus recognised in Christ have nothing in common with a nirmanakaya. If the passage from the *Parinibbana-sutta* from which we started can be looked upon as tending already towards the illusionism, or at least the relativism, sanctioned in the Great Vehicle by the idea of nirmanakaya, our Patristic texts remain no less certainly in the traditional line of *Verbum caro factum*. Compare them, for instance, with *Mahaprajnaparamitasastra*, 34: ". . . In each of the other Jambudvipas they say: Our Buddha is the true Buddha, the Buddhas of the other worlds are simply imitations."[40] It is clear that from one point of view there is a common parentage, but no less obviously the movement of thought is the exact opposite.[41]

II

"SAMBHOGAKAYA" AND TRANSFIGURATION

(i) *The Divine Apparition in Philo*

The doctrine stated sporadically in the Pali Canon, particularly in the passage we have quoted from the *Mahaparinibbana-sutta*, is developed much more fully in the Mahayana at about the beginning of the first century A.D. In the theory of the Trikaya, i.e. the Buddha's three bodies, it becomes a complete system which includes an entire cosmology and metaphysic. In the classic form of the theory the three "bodies" are distinguished and arranged in a hierarchy: nirmanakaya, sambhogakaya, dharmakaya.[42]

Now the speculations on the sambhogakaya contain passages which can be compared with passages to be found in the writings of the Alexandrians and the Gnostics.

As the middle term of the series, sambhogakaya has as its first general characteristic the fact that it is perceptible by the Bodhisattvas alone, i.e. by beings who are already ripe for salvation. In exactly the same way we find in Philo a queer apparition who is to guide the faithful Jews at the time of the coming of the Kingdom: "Then those who previously were dispersed will tend with one accord, each from his own side, towards the appointed place, guided by an Apparition more divine than human, an Apparition invisible to others and manifest only to those who are to be saved."[43]

Obviously, this is an allusion to the column of fire that guided the Israelites in the desert. Nevertheless, this mysterious Being remains difficult to identify. Some people (for instance, Döhnea) have seen in this passage—quite wrongly, apparently —a reference to the Messias. Fr. Lagrange first believed that it referred to an angel, who would become a guide appearing "in less humble conditions than those under which the angel Gabriel" appeared in the Book of Tobias:[44] then he decided that it represented "something like what was seen by Daniel in a vision, a son of man coming upon the clouds".[45] According to Grégoire, who has thoroughly examined the whole question, it seems more probable that it describes the Logos.[46] In any case, particularly if the latter hypothesis is correct, there is a genuine connection between it and the Buddhist idea.

(ii) Passages from Origen on the Transfiguration

Still more striking, however, is the following connection, once again with Origen.

Apart from other characteristics, which have no parallel with anything Christian, the sambhogakaya is a "body of glory". According to Masson-Oursel, "it has the appearance of a shining meteor, similar to the beatific bodies of the saints of Christianity, or even to the glorified body of Christ".[47] But this appearance does not involve any absolute quality; it has no existence "in itself", apart from a certain relationship. Like the nirmanakaya at a lower level, the sambhogakaya arises from a collaboration between the appearance and the person who contemplates it; so that, having no solidity—and even, in point of fact, no real existence at all—apart from this relationship, it varies every time the connection between the two terms, the seen and the seer, changes. It is therefore always subject to an indefinite virtual multiplicity. In other words, because, on this hypothesis, the "seen" remains in itself both unchanged and inaccessible in its secret essence or its pure "emptiness", therefore the sambhogakaya can assume successively, or even simultaneously, a variety of forms, according to the nature, dignity, spiritual elevation, "degree of being" or degree of perfection of each "seer".[48] And the prototype of all these "bodies of glory" is the glorified Sakyamuni as shown in The Lotus of the Good Law, preaching the transcendent Law to his chosen disciples on Mount Gridhrakuta.[49] Now listen to Origen in his *Commentary on St. Matthew*, explaining the transfiguration of Christ on the mountain before His three chosen disciples:

"And after six days Jesus taketh with him Peter and James and John his brother and bringeth them up into a high mountain apart, and he was transfigured before them" (Matt. xvii. 1–2; Mark ix. 1).

. . . If any one of us wishes to be taken by Jesus and brought up into the high mountain and to be made worthy of seeing Him transfigured in a lonely place, he must first spend six whole days paying no attention to visible things, feeling no affection for the world or anything in it . . . no desire for anything that may distract the soul from divine things. Then, full of joy, he will celebrate a new sabbath, on the high mountain, and see Jesus transfigured before his eyes. For the Logos has various forms, appearing to each person in the measure suitable to him, and not allowing Himself to be seen by anyone beyond what he can bear.[50]

You may perhaps be wondering whether, when Jesus was transfigured before those whom He had taken up into the high mountain, He allowed Himself to be seen of them in the form of God which He had in the beginning; whether, as He appeared in the form of a slave to those who remained in the plain, He appeared, not in this form, but in the form of God to those who had followed Him for six days up the high mountain.

Well, if you can, you must understand this in an entirely spiritual way. For it does not merely say: "He was transfigured", but there is something essential added to this both by Matthew and by Mark. In both their Gospels, in fact, it is written: "He was transfigured before them". This most certainly authorises you to say that Jesus can at one and the same moment be transfigured in this way before some and not before others.[51]

There are many other passages in Origen which develop this idea. He returns to it particularly in the *Contra Celsum*, in which he replies to various objections made by Celsus; as, for example, in the second book, Chapter LXIV:

Jesus, though in Himself a simple unity, was multiple according to the knowledge that people had of Him, and He was not seen by all in the same way.

That He did not always appear the same to the people who saw Him, but appeared to them according to their capacity, will be quite clearly recognised by anyone who remembers that before being transfigured upon the mountain he did not take with Him all His apostles, but only Peter, James and John, these being the only ones who were capable of contemplating His glory . . . And when Judas, wishing to deliver Him up, said to those who accompanied Him: "Whomsoever I shall kiss, that same is He," thus giving the impression that they would not have recognised Jesus: this also seems to prove that Jesus did not always have the same appearance. The Saviour Himself appears to suggest this when He says: "I was with you daily in the temple and ye took Me not . . ." Believing, therefore, that Jesus, not only as to His inner divinity which was hidden from many, but even as to His body, whose appearance He changed at will and before whomsoever He would . . .[52]

And again, in the sixth book, Chapter LXXVII:

When Celsus writes: "From the moment that the divine Spirit willed to assume a body, it was absolutely necessary that this body should be above all others in its splendour, its beauty, its strength, its majesty and its eloquence", why could he not see that this body was indeed above all others in that it appeared to each person as it was bound to appear to him according to his capacity and his needs?

And there is no cause for astonishment in the fact that matter, which is indeterminate by nature, able to clothe any form whatsoever at the will of the Creator and infinitely malleable in the hands of its divine Workman, should at one time be given a quality that occasioned the words: "He had neither form nor comeliness", and at another a different quality, so glorious, so splendid, so marvellous, that the three apostles who had ascended the mountain with Jesus fell on their faces at the sight of such beauty.

It must be added that this doctrine has a mystical meaning: The various appearances assumed by Jesus symbolise the nature of the divine Logos, who does not reveal Himself in the same way to the crowd as He does to those who are able to follow Him on to the high mountain of which we have been speaking.[53]

To explain these metamorphoses, Origen, as can be seen, alludes to a theory of the plasticity of matter to which he often had recourse.[54] This idea was quite a common one. It is here only introduced in a subsidiary manner, to justify against an opponent an idea that has been reached on other grounds; but its application in this case of the Transfiguration is no less interesting on that account.[55]

As an intermediary—a changeable and purely relative intermediary—between the "form of God" and the "form of a slave", this "transfigured body", which is such only to those whose eyes are adapted to it, is a near relative—at least when abstracted from a considerable context of doctrine—to that other intermediary between the inaccessible dharmakaya and the common nirmanakaya—the sambhogakaya. And the "high mountain" in Palestine, transformed into a mystic height inaccessible to the vulgar crowd, likewise calls to mind that other height near to the Indian town of Rajagriha, which was also the seat of the celestial Assembly to which the followers of the despised Hinayana were unable to attain: the Mount Gridhrakuta of "The Lotus". [56]

(iii) Before Origen

Despite the fact that Origen refers to the actual words of Matthew and Mark in his account of the Transfiguration, it is obvious that the Gospels, taken by themselves, are not sufficient to account for this idea. Nor was Origen himself the originator of it. He is content to make use of it, either to explain a text from the Gospels or to reply to the objections of Celsus, or to develop his own spiritual teaching. He makes it his own without any effort; he certainly has no scruples about using it. But, as he himself says, he received it from tradition: "A tradition has come down to us, that there were not only two forms in Christ, one being the form in which everybody saw Him and the other the form into which He was transfigured before His disciples on the mountain, when His face shone like the sun; but He appeared to each person in the form that they were worthy to see Him."[57]

Labourt and Batiffol, in their edition of the Canticle of Canticles, associate this with a passage from Clement of Alexandria which refers to another tradition, clearly Docetist, that the body of Christ was supposed not to have offered any resistance to the sense of touch;[58] but though these two ideas may indeed have some connection with each other by way of a general atmosphere of thought, or rather imagination, it seems to me that it would be a mistake to consider them identical.[59] More nearly approximating to Origen is another fragment preserved by Clement in the *Excerpta ex Theodoto*.[60] In this the author, who seems to be Clement himself, admires "the great humility" of the Lord, which enabled Him to appear "not as an angel, but as a man"; then he goes on to make clear that it was not with their fleshly eyes that the apostles saw the radiance of Christ transfigured; for the eyes, he says, have nothing in common with such a light except in the measure conceded to them by the compassion of the Saviour. [61]

The *Excerpta ex Theodoto* are not by any means the only evidence of the tradition referred to by Origen. There is no space here to mention all the comparable passages in the Christian literature before Origen, or to embark on any comparative study of them, or for any attempt at a genealogical list of them. [62] Their family likeness seems often merely a result of the fact that identical phrases recur in different contexts, expressing quite different doctrines. The meaning of these phrases varies according to the application of them made by each author. The most interesting example of this is perhaps to be found in St. Irenaeus, who on the one hand uses the phrase "juvenis et senex", the very phrase used in the *Acts of John*, whilst on the other hand he vigorously combats the doctrine expressed in the *Acts of John* by this phrase. [63] In these passages it is sometimes the Logos who is being described in His successive manifestations, and sometimes only Christ in His life on earth; sometimes it is the Transfiguration, and sometimes later visions granted to favoured ones amongst the faithful; sometimes the author merely seems to be aiming to stress the idea of the divine condescension, and sometimes he seems to teach a more or less radical Docetism. What is more important for us to notice, however, is that, as Origen expressly says, we are here faced with a tradition.

Origen may have read in the *Acts of Peter* the following explanation of the Incarnation, put into the mouth of the apostle himself as a prologue to his account of the scene in which Jesus was transfigured: "In those days error had spread abroad and many thousands were plunging into perdition. Then, impelled by His divine compassion, the Lord manifested Himself in another form, and appeared in the image of a man whom neither the Jews nor we can worthily describe. For each one of us could only see Him as he was able, according to his capacity for seeing."

There follows a brief description of the Transfiguration, [64] which ends again with the words, "iterum talem eum vidi, qualem capere potui" (I saw him again, to the extent that I was able), and Peter ends his speech by reciting the Saviour's many appellations. Then, the assembly having begun to pray, there is a blinding light, and Jesus appears to a number of widows who have just come to believe in Him: some see Him as a child, others as a youth, others as an old man. [65]

In this account, as in many others, the *Acts of Peter* depend very closely, perhaps through the *Acts of Paul*, on the *Acts of John*, whose Docetism is here, however, considerably mitigated. [66] The idea presented by Origen existed therefore long before he did, and in a more radical form, for the *Acts of Peter* apply it to the whole activity of the Saviour on earth. [67] Its Gnostic connections are not disputed, and it may be remembered in this connection that (according to St. Irenaeus) the one great Gnostic on whom Buddhist influence is, on other grounds, the most likely—Basilides—maintained that Christ, being a *virtus incorporalis*, could transform Himself at will and at will make Himself invisible. [68]

(iv) The Δυνάμεις of Philo

In our pursuit of these two ideas of the transfigured body and the Word as "an angel amongst the angels", we have gone back into an earlier Christian age before Origen and into a "Gnostic" atmosphere. It seems possible to go back even further and discover a pre-Christian form of this idea, still without leaving the Alexandrian circle. Philo's idea of the δυνάμεις is closely related to the idea of the sambhogakaya. Here, for instance, is how Henri-Charles Puech explains Philo's idea, without having any intention of making the kind of comparison we have in mind: ". . . In my opinion the Powers do not represent elements or aspects of the divine essence itself so much as forms assumed by God in the eyes of the creature at the various stages of the mystical ascension. They are 'relative' points of view adopted towards the supreme Ὄν, which only have meaning in and through the various relationships which man is able to have with God."[69]

Furthermore, this idea was not, even at that time, a product of any spontaneous imagination, either Jewish or Christian; it was rooted in ancient traditions, some quite archaic, of which no doubt a trace is to be found in the biblical reference to "the angel of Jahweh", in the account of Gedeon's vocation,[70] and in the apparitions which came to Manue and his wife before Samson was born.[71]

(v) Speculations on the Manna

More immediately, the same idea was rooted in Alexandrian traditions—traditions about the manna, of which the first hint is to be found in the Book of Wisdom:

> *Thou didst feed they people with the food of angels,*
> *And gavest them bread from heaven, prepared without labour,*
> *Having in it all that is delicious and the sweetness of every taste.*
> *For thy sustenance showed thy sweetness to thy children,*
> *And serving every man's will,*
> *It was turned to what every man liked.*[72]

This theme had quickly been developed. The various subjective tastes procured by the manna had been described in detail and more or less "objectified"; then the marvellous properties of this bodily food had been taken as symbolic of the marvellous properties of the Logos, the spiritual food of souls.

The Jewish traditions about the manna are mentioned in passing by St. Basil, who quotes Philo in a *Letter to Amphilochus*:[73]

In his explanation of the manna, Philo, apparently following a Jewish tradition, said that its quality was of such a nature that it changed according to the imagination of the person who ate it. In itself it was said to be like a grain of wheat cooked in honey. But it could take the place either of honey or of meat, and this meat could be the flesh of bird or animal. Sometimes it tasted like a vegetable and sometimes like a fish.

Now these two traditions concerning the various flavours of the manna and the various physical appearances of Christ are connected explicitly, again by Origen. In the passage from the *Series* on St. Matthew, c. 100, whose opening lines we have already quoted, he goes on:

> He appeared to each person in the form in which each deserved to see Him. And whilst always Himself He was never seen by any as Himself. As it is written of the manna, which God sent down to the sons of Israel—a heavenly bread, having every kind of flavour and pleasing to every palate, which was submissive to the desire of whosoever ate it and was transformed into whatsoever he desired.
>
> And this tradition does not seem to me to be beyond belief, either concerning Jesus Himself as envisaged in the body, revealing Himself to men under different aspects, or as it concerns the nature of the Logos Himself, who does not transmit Himself to all in the same way. [74]

Contrariwise, in the *Seventh Homily on Exodus* the subject of the manna leads to a discussion of the Lord who willed to become flesh and bread for us: [75]

> "*In the evening you shall eat flesh, and in the morning you shall have your fill of bread*" (Exodus xvi. 12). And, in truth, we for whom "the Word was made flesh" in the last days and in the evening of the world, say that the Lord makes Himself known to us in the flesh which He received from the Virgin. . . . For us the Word of God is also bread (and we eat it each morning) because He is the Sun of Justice, who causes a new light to shine on those who believe in him.
>
> . . . And do not be astonished that the Word of God should be described as flesh and bread and even as vegetable, that

He should be named differently according to the measure of the faithful and the capacity of those who receive Him. At this time, when we are still at the beginning of things, we cannot eat the pure flesh of the Word, i.e. we are not yet capable of the consummate and perfect doctrine. . . .

Thus, therefore, the manna of the Word of God produces whatever flavour you like in your mouth. . . . And whereas this manna is like the sweetest ·honey to the faithful, to the unfaithful it becomes a worm.[76]

This theme, in which echoes of St. Paul are to be heard, had already been developed by Clement. The Father, Clement had said in his *Paedagogus*,[77] gives men the Logos as food. To some He is milk; to others He is a solid food; but His substance is always the same: thus were the ancient Hebrews fed with manna, the bread of heaven. Origen returns to this again and again; on such a topic he is inexhaustible. He deals with it again in the *Contra Celsum*:

Of the nature of the Logos I say that, as food changes into milk inside the mother to suit the nature of the child, and as doctors prepare food in one way for sick people and in another way for those who are well, so God transforms the power of the Logos, who is made to feed the human soul,[78] according to the condition of each separate person. To one, as Scripture says, the Logos becomes "reasonable milk, without admixture"; to another, still weak in the Faith, He becomes a strengthening oil; to the perfect He is solid food. And yet the Logos never deceives as to His true nature by thus feeding each person according to his needs. There is in Him neither lying nor deceit: οὐ πλανᾷ, οὐδὲ ψεύδεται.[79]

(vi) The Saving Lie
This last passage provides a little lesson in prudence which we may be forgiven for mentioning in passing.

At first sight it seems remarkable that the words with which this passage ends should be exactly the same words as are used by the Buddha Sakyamuni, in "The Lotus of the Good Law", to conclude his teaching on the upaya, i.e. the "tricks", "the cleverness in the use of means", the "saving subterfuges", which the Buddhas use to suit their teaching and even their very appearance to the condition of each individual being. There is a curious similarity in both the situation and the idea, and in the expression of the idea. "Knowing our miserable inclinations", seeing us immersed "in the filth of desire", the Buddhas know that they cannot "establish us immediately in the treasure-house of their knowledge", and so "by means of a singularly surprising miracle" they devote themselves to "proportioning their teaching to the strength of each hearer", in order to lead us all to the desired end. They do not, therefore, all say the same thing. But if their words are enigmatic we must not conclude that they are deceitful: "O Sariputra, he tells no lie, the venerable Tathagata who declares the truth that is excellent; but his language is difficult to grasp. Why is this? It is because, to explain the Law, he cleverly uses different means . . . aiming to lead all beings to maturity and conversion. . . . Therefore there is nothing untruthful in what he says. . . . O men of wisdom, do not doubt it: the Word which I utter is true. Never, never, is it anything but the truth."[80]

But the whole interest of this passage immediately evaporates when, going back a few lines in the *Contra Celsum*, we discover that in the words he uses at the end of his explanation Origen is only repeating the expressions used by Celsus himself: by making Himself seem to change when He does not change, says Celsus to the Christians, your God "is a deceiver and a liar", πλανᾷ καὶ ψεύδεται.

In any case, in his reply to Celsus, Origen has a wider aim; for here, as in other passages,[81] he is suggesting a whole criticism of mythology as being always untruthful, even when it apes the truth, whilst the Logos is always Truth, even when He seems temporarily to assume the appearance of untruth.[82]

For the Word of God is not like anyone else's speech; as His anger is not like anyone else's anger, so neither is His deceit like anyone else's deceit: man will always have to recognise in the end that following the voice of God, at whatever stage it may be, always means following the voice of Truth which will lead him to salvation. Leaving aside certain analogies with the thought of Plato which have often been commented on, Origen thus stands in vigorous opposition to the Hellenism with which he was faced. He nevertheless developed a whole theory of what may be described as the instructive lie of salvation, or the "economy of the lie", a theory which fundamentally has far more resemblance to The Lotus of the Good Law than to Plato. Therefore, though the connection between the two expressions quoted above is illusory and there is no sign of any bond between them, the case nevertheless seems worth mentioning as an example of a very remarkable analogy of ideas, even though it is far from being complete.[83]

(vii) The Spiritual Transposition

The last two passages from Origen (taken from On Exodus and Against Celsus) are interesting for another reason. We now leave all theories concerning the appearances assumed by Christ in His fleshly or transfigured body, and speculations on the nature of matter or sensible perception. All we are concerned with now is the union of the soul with the Word; the eyes of the soul which with varying degrees of perspicuity pierce the human "envelope" to the Word, or the Word which enters the soul to different degrees of depth, enlightening and feeding it. We are now concerned with one thing only: the mystery of the inner life. And, quite clearly, this is the essential idea, the one idea above all others with which this great man of the spirit was concerned; to this leads each of the passages mentioned earlier:[84] "This doctrine has a mystical meaning":[85]

To those who remain below [on the mountain], and who are not yet in a proper state to ascend, this Word has . . .

"no form nor comeliness"; they can see nothing in it which is not worthy of scorn; they regard it as being a great deal inferior to the words of other men, here described figuratively as "the children of men". In truth it can be said that the words of the philosophers, which are simply human productions, seem a good deal finer than the Word of God, which when preached to the People presents the mind with "the folly of preaching", and which, because of this apparent folly, makes those who judge it simply by its appearance say: "We have seen it; it has no form nor comeliness." But to those who have the strength to follow it and to accompany it up into the high mountain, to them it has a beauty altogether divine, a beauty which can only be discovered by those like Peter who have within themselves the edifice of the Church, built upon the Word of God; who have become so habituated to the good that not one of the Gates of Hell can ever prevail against them . . . if, again, they have been reborn through the Word, if their voice is full of virtue, and if they are in no way inferior to those who have merited to be called the Sons of Thunder.[86]

The same idea, resulting from a similar transposition, is to be found in many comparable passages, for example in the lovely *Third Homily on St. Luke*, in which it appears, so to speak, in a pure state:

Things which are physical and lacking in reason do nothing to make themselves visible to others, and yet if the eye of another is turned on them, it sees whatever is in its line of vision, whether they want it or not. For what person or thing, which is limited by solid flesh, can do anything to make itself invisible to those present?

On the other hand, things which are celestial and sacred, need not be seen if they do not want to be, even when they are present. It is for them to choose whether they want to be seen or not. It was by God's grace that He appeared to

Abraham or the other prophets. It was not just because Abraham could see with his soul that he saw God; it was also because God by His grace made Himself visible to a just man.

This should be understood not only with regard to God the Father but to God the Saviour and to God the Holy Ghost as well, and to lesser spirits, such as the cherubim and seraphim. And we are not only talking about "this generation", but about the future too. For when we have left this world, God and the angels will not be visible to all of us. . . .

This should be understood concerning Christ, when He appeared in the flesh. For many who saw Him were not capable really of seeing Him. In fact they only saw His body; they could not see Him for what He really was, the Christ . . . they only saw Jesus in so far as He judged them worthy of His sight.

Let us strive, then, that God may show Himself in our presence. For the holy word of Scripture has promised that "although He may be discovered by those who do not feel Him, He only appears to those who believe in Him.[87]

The same idea appears in the *Commentary on St. Matthew*: "Perhaps the word of God appears in different kinds of glory, according to the state of each soul that sees Him";[88] or in the *Commentary on Canticles*: when the crowd was pressing upon Christ only the woman who made Him turn round "touched" Him; in the same way, of those who looked at Him, only those who were worthy to see Him "saw" Him—and the Father in Him.[89] For He is in reality invisible to anyone who does not possess the eyes of the spirit, the eyes of faith.[90] And the various ἐπίνοιαι which are to be distinguished in Him are, in reality, simply so many glimpses of Him, so many points of view adopted towards Him according to the degree of progress made towards perfection in the spiritual life.[91]

Breathing the atmosphere of Alexandria, Origen received

from it some curious ideas which may have come from the heart of India; he expresses these just as they came to him and may very well have taken them literally;[92] but almost at once he gives them a new shade of meaning, a new inflexion, he puts his mark upon them—the mark of the Christian, systematising them and at the same time rendering them objective; extracting their spiritual meaning. In him the Gnostic heritage is purified and transposed into an order of spiritual significance, so that, filtered, softened, spiritualised, interiorised, it is then ready to enter into the main stream of Christian tradition. In proof of this we need only quote here the names of two great figures, who were both undoubtedly influenced by Origen, St. Gregory of Nyssa and St. Bernard. Gregory of Nyssa was to say in his *Third Homily on the Canticle of Canticles*:

In each person who receives Him, the Child Jesus who has been born to us grows differently in wisdom, age, and grace; He is not the same in all, but appears according to the capacity of each person who carries Him, either as a child, or as a youth, or in His maturity.[93] [St. Bernard refers more than once to the various ways in which the Word, who is in Himself unchanging, appears to men according to their spiritual disposition and the degree to which they are prepared to receive Him.[94] Using the same metaphor in the contrary sense, he also speaks of the Lord's single appearance:] While Christ always remains the same in Himself, nevertheless the vision of Him which you see is not always of equal efficacy but is partnered by the merits of the individuals whom He looks upon, striking fear into some, and bringing comfort to others.[95]

There can be no question, in passages of this kind, of any esotericism or Docetism; *a fortiori*, there can be no question of any connection with the sambhogakaya. These passages are nevertheless related to others whose thought, it must be confessed, has sufficient resemblance to Buddhist theories to raise the question of a common source or a borrowing by one or the other.[96]

(viii) The Unique Sun

There is one final analogy to be noted. At the end of a penetrating analysis of the prefix *sam*, combined with a comparison with the relevant data in the Little Vehicle, Paul Mus comes to the conclusion that sambhogakaya should be translated as "communal body", or "body of common fruition". The word would then suggest either the intimate union between the Buddhas at the moment before their fusion in the ineffable unity of the dharmakaya, or the union of the Bodhisattvas in the blessedness of the "pure land"—which is itself sometimes called the "land of sambhoga". Gaining one's own sambhoga would therefore mean, according to the communal theory of the Little Vehicle, having access to the one single, glorious Assembly; having one's own individual share, if one may still put it thus, in the collective sambhogakaya—svasambhogakaya, according to the terminology later to be used by Hiuan Tsang; it would mean entering in the fullest sense into communion with the body of the elect, who no longer possess anything to themselves, and where there is no longer "any idea of self and others", as the *Mahasukhavativyuha* says. Therefore, there is at once glory and communion: the sambhogakaya, Fa-hien was to say, has its own centre, like the sun.[97] Asanga,[98] one of the great theorists of the trikaya, had written: "Just as an infinite number of rays mingle in the face of the sun, all having the same function of lighting the world, so, in the 'scheme of peace', an infinite number of Buddhas mingle in one single occupation."

A day will come, says Origen, likewise, "when the just will shine in their Father's Kingdom, becoming a single sun". And a little further on he says: ". . . until all are consummated in one perfect man, and become a single sun. Then they will shine like the sun in their Father's Kingdom".[99]

No doubt Origen is here simply expressing an idea common enough in the Christian faith, and one which despite appearances is utterly different from the Buddhist idea. Not infrequently, two doctrines may be not only different but utterly opposed, and yet, seen from a particular angle, or with each reduced to one of its elements, resemble each other so closely—especially if they happen to share a common metaphor—that they seem identical. Such appearances, however superficial they may be, are not always entirely illusory: they are themselves facts and may indicate a real contact and exchange of ideas. It is not therefore entirely irrelevant to note here too the similarity between these Buddhist phrases and the phrases used by Origen, although, generally speaking, the symbol of the sun is not peculiar to either.[100]

III

THE BUDDHA LOKOTTARA

(i) *The Seven Steps of the Buddha*

We have already had occasion to refer to the *Acts* of Peter, Paul and John. The last-mentioned contain another passage which has its analogy in Buddhism. The Apostle is recalling his memories of Christ. "When I walked with Him," he says, "I often used to try to see whether His feet left any imprint on the ground, for I had noticed that as He walked he was raised above it; and I could see absolutely nothing."[101] This is obviously mentioned as a sign of the supernatural character which, according to these Acts, was possessed by Christ. The Christ who is represented here would not have been able to say, with the author of the Book of Wisdom: "And being born, I drew in the common air, and fell upon the earth, that is made alike; and the first voice which I uttered was crying, as all others do."[102] Now the same thing occurs in Buddhist legend, according to which Sakyamuni too never touched the ground.

From the very beginning, in his mother's womb, he was protected from any contact with impurity by a covering of precious
stones. At his birth a miraculous lotus held him aloft, or,
according to other versions of the legend, the gods caught him
in a golden net, or else they spread out underneath him the
skin of an antelope or a tiger, or some precious material.[103]
. . . Throughout his existence lotus flowers sprang up under
each step that he took; the ground became level without his
touching it: "Wherever the lord of the world goes, the low
places are raised and the high places become flat . . . The
plant of his feet is not stained by dust."[104] These symbols
express the idea that the Buddha is "lokottara", i.e. "above
the world".[105] But there is no need to assume that the *Acts
of John*, or the religious circles from which they derived,
depended on any Buddhist source for this point; they may easily
have been influenced by the ceremonial traditionally belonging to the Pharaohs, just as the legend about the Buddha who
is lokottara—often a royal Buddha, a "Buddha adorned"—
may have developed from the ritual connected with Indian
royalty.[106]

The point which concerns us at the moment is that the explanations of these legends about the Buddha given by Paul
Mus, in his *Barabudur*, may perhaps help us to understand the
passage from the *Acts of John*; for we can now connect it with a
passage from the work of another Christian apocryphal writer,
the *Proto-Gospel of James*. It concerns the child Mary:

From day to day the child grew in strength. And when
she was six months old, her mother set her upon the ground
to see whether she could stand up. And having taken seven
steps forward, the child returned to her mother's lap, and
her mother, lifting her up, said: "Long live the Lord my
God! You must not walk on this earth [ἐν τῇ γῇ ταύτῃ]
until I take you to the Temple of the Lord." And she made a
sanctuary in her chamber, and nothing that was impure or
unclean did she allow the child to touch.[107]

If the only reference in this passage was to the raising of the child from the ground, one would merely be reminded of the analogy with the old Roman goddess who was called *dea Levana* because she lifted up every new-born child from the ground—as is explained by St. Augustine on the authority of Varro.[108] But there is also a reference to "seven steps". Now these seven steps are an essential element in the legend about the child Siddharta. There are many variants of the story, which is a heritage from the old Vedic mythology.[109] Sometimes the steps are taken in one direction only, the north,[110] at others in four, six, or even ten directions, but one thing is never missed out, and that is the seven steps. Again, sometimes the feet of the new-born child rest flat on the ground, which seems to be raised and made level by them without their needing to be supported by it; sometimes they are raised above the ground to a height of four inches, and sometimes they come to rest at each step upon a lotus;[111] but these are merely slight variations of one unchanging symbol. Here is how Ashvaghosha expresses it in his *Buddhacarita*, a poem about the life of the Buddha: "The Bodhisattva, like the stars of the Seven Wise Men [i.e. the Great Bear], took seven steps forward, calmly and resolutely, and under each step appeared a lotus; neither crushing nor lengthy were these seven steps."[112]

"Everywhere lotus flowers sprang up under his feet," Nagarjuna was to write,[113] "at each step a great lotus sprang up under his feet."

The "magic levelling", the birth of the protective lotus, the elevation above the ground—all mean the same thing: all signify the Buddha's ability to walk along raised from the ground, and this, as Paul Mus has shown, is closely connected with the theme of the seven steps.[114] Both are signs of the Buddha who is lokottara (supra-mundane, "hyper-cosmic", supernatural). The Buddha no sooner came into the world than with seven "symbolic strides" he sprang up above the world, ascending the steps of the cosmic pyramid as though mounting a giant ladder with seven rungs, each marked by a lotus.[115] Now in the *Proto-Gospel of James* we find the same two themes associated, though their meaning, in so far as it can be discerned, seems to have become more commonplace. Is one to conclude that this is no more than a curious coincidence?

(ii) Docetism

The *Acts of John*, as we have said, issued from a circle which was strongly Docetist in tone. Similarly, these legendary characteristics attributed to the Buddha who is "lokottara" or "supernatural" are Docetist doctrines. It would be instructive to pursue the parallel between the various forms of "Christian" and Buddhist Docetism; the explanations, sometimes even the very words, are identical on both sides. Thus, for instance, one reads in the *Mahavastu*, which expounds the Buddhology of the Lokottaravadins: "In the Buddhas everything was supernatural" (lokottara—$\dot{v}\pi\varepsilon\rho\kappa o\sigma\mu\acute{i}o\nu$, *supramundanum*),[116] whilst in Philoxenus of Mabbogh, a Syriac author of the fifth century, one finds these words: "In Christ everything was supernatural."[117] Nevertheless, the two remarks have very different meanings; for whereas what is meant in the *Mahavastu* is that "the Buddhas are not in any sense created by their mother and father", since they have "absolutely nothing in common with the world",[118] Philoxenus of Mabbogh is simply using a number of paradoxical distinctions to assert the natural incorruptibility of the body of Christ, so as to be able to lay more emphasis on the voluntary nature of His death.

The fact is that, taking the matter as a whole, besides the similar variations that are developed on this subject, a contrary process is to be observed in the two religions. The thing which in Christianity began by being, and went on being, a heresy, sapping the very basis of the faith, became increasingly in Buddhism, in accordance with the very nature of Indian thought, the orthodoxy of a considerable proportion of Buddhism.[119] Thus one of the reasons why Ananda, Sakyamuni's beloved disciple, was so roughly handled by later tradition, was because of the simple way he had taken pity on his master's bodily infirmities.[120] And whereas, in its effort to get itself recognised, Christian Docetism was obliged to take on increasingly attenuated forms, Buddhist Docetism grew more and more exaggerated. For Marcion, for example, the body of Christ was pure appearance, but even for his disciple Apelles it had become a real body which Christ had manufactured for Himself for the occasion from cosmic elements.[121] Soon Christian Docetism was hardly able to survive except in the most diluted forms, barely to be distinguished from those of Christian orthodoxy—as can be seen in certain tendencies in the Christology of St. Hilary.[122] In Buddhism the process was the exact opposite. The germs of Docetism which Buddhism carried within itself developed to a prodigious extent. The deeper one delves into the history of Buddhism, the more one finds it invaded by a radical, universal Docetism. The marvellous circumstances surrounding the baby Siddharta's arrival on earth are no more than the first stage in this process. However little the body of the future Buddha was supposed to have been truly "born", this was soon found by the Mahayana to be unworthy of a perfect Buddha. At the moment of Bodhi a miraculous substitution must therefore have taken place.[123] But even this was not sufficient. They began by saying, more or less, "From the night of Bodhi to the night of Nirvana the Buddha did not utter a single word" (Candrakirti)—because his physical body, "the body with which he was born", the vehicle of speech, was thereafter merely appearance, having actually been exchanged for a "Buddha body", an "Essential" or "Diamond body". They ended by saying: "The Buddha never came into the world", "The Buddha never taught the Dharma", because the body which appeared on earth and which could speak had never been anything but appearance, "a fictitious body", nirmanakaya.[124] The Buddha may "appear to men as an ordinary man"; it nevertheless remains true that "his body is indescribable and surpasses all the worlds".[125]

(iii) *"Semel locutus est"*

As developed in the Great Vehicle, Buddhist Docetism is not merely a way of explaining the body and person of the Buddha. It becomes part of a vast idealist system, or rather, the explanation itself develops into a vast idealist system, to which, obviously, nothing comparable can be found in the Christian tradition. This does not mean, however, that partial resemblances may not be discovered here too. We shall conclude our discussion with a reference to two of them. They take us still further beyond the limits of the Alexandrian circle, from which we have already begun to draw away.

The explanations already given have by no means exhausted the meaning of the saying, "The Buddha never taught the Dharma". Just as the body of the Buddha which is seen by men and devas, and even by the Bodhisattvas, is never, according to Mahayanist idealism, anything more than appearance, so the letter of his Dharma too, the whole collection of instructions, the mass of scriptures composing the canon—including both the Great and Little Vehicles—is entirely superficial. Behind this letter, which in itself is no more than ruta—sound, noise—and whose only value is as a sign—vyanjana—one must therefore look for the meaning—artha—in which alone is to be found the "Refuge".[126] "The Word of the Buddha is different from the letter."[127] From this letter and all its multiplicity one must therefore rise to the unity of the Dharma in its Essence, the only real "Word of Buddha". He never utters any other. This unique Word, "in which inequality has no place", is never-ending. Those who are enslaved by their desires can no more hear it than deaf people can hear thunder;[128] those who are beginning to purify themselves can see in it the instructions concerning the Ten Defences; to those who have subjugated their passions it teaches nirvana.[129] But in itself it remains always "homogeneous, complete and pure".

This is explained explicitly in the "Lotus":

My blessing for an inconceivable number of Kalpas has always been that which I have just given; and I never leave this spot on the summit of the Gridhrakuta and go and take my seat on any other of the myriad resting-places . . .

There are beings who go for innumerable Kalpas without even hearing the name of Tathagata or of the Law; this is the result of their guilty deeds.

But when it happens that beings full of gentleness and loving-kindness are born, they are no sooner in the world than as a result of their virtuous conduct they see me engaged in explaining the Law.[130]

Now this pure teaching, this unique Word, is one with the Teacher, with the Buddha himself.

Enlarging our horizon still further, we find ourselves obliged to extend this principle for the explanation of the sacred texts to the explanation of everything that exists. In all things we have to pass from the level of relative truth or "concealed truth" or "truth in error" (samvrti), which is accessible and multiple and perfectly apparent, to the level of absolute truth (paramartha), which is ineffable in its unity.[131] Thus, once again we discover the unique Dharma, which is the principle of the universe as well as the law of salvation. The lower level is not of course pure illusion, any more than the letter of the sacred writings is untrue: both are upayas, contrived for us by the condescension of the Buddhas because of our weakness, which they wish to remedy. In neither case, however, is it properly speaking their own work or word; for if the Dharma remains essentially ineffable, this is not simply because of our present imperfection; it is because it is essentially Emptiness. "The Bodhisattvas who turn aside from Emptiness are turning away from the whole of the Great Vehicle."[132] The truth is that "the Buddha never taught the Dharma" to the Bodhisattvas any more than he taught it to devas or men. He has never left his state of perfect composure. Hence no essential Word has ever been heard: the Emptiness of the Dharma has never been the object of any ontological affirmation.

The analogies with certain Christian neo-Platonist speculations on the Logos are clearly evident. There is the same idea of the condescension of an instructor explaining the whole development of the way of salvation and the whole luxuriant variety of the scriptures. There is the same distinction—taking the thing as a whole, at least—between the letter and the spirit of the sacred book, between the letter which is multiple, accessible to people immersed in the multiplicity of this world, and the spirit which reduces everything to the unity in which alone salvation is to be found. There is the same connection between this scriptural symbolism and the idea of a universal symbolism, in which the "logoi" hidden in everything lead to the unique Logos—so that there are many Fathers of the Church who could quote the Buddhist saying: "If I point to anything, it is foolish to look at my finger instead of looking in the direction in which I am pointing."[133] And there is the same identification of the Logos who is to be found at the heart of the scriptures with the Being who comes in human form to bring salvation to men; both being in the same sense, without any duality, the Word.[134]

Nevertheless, there is one difference which affects all the rest. Even when the kinship is closest, the contrast remains absolute. No doubt the multiplicity of the saving words is no more proper to God or to His Logos considered as God, according to Christian neo-Platonism, than in the Mahayana it is proper to the Buddha and his Dharma. But whereas, according to the latter, the Buddha has never really spoken, any more than he has ever really manifested himself to men— for the Dharma is empty, just as the universe is empty—according to the Christian teaching God utters from all eternity a Word in which He expresses himself fully: *Semel locutus est Deus.*[135] On the Christian side only does affirmation triumph. Both at the beginning and at the end of everything there is, not an empty Dharma, but a substantial Word. *In principio erat Verbum*. And the revelation of this unique Word to men is real, its incarnation amongst men is real. *Et Verbum caro factum est*. One can therefore say again, quite truly, that the multiplicity of the sayings which are necessary in order to conceive the Word is entirely relative to men: *Semel locutus est Deus, et plura audita sunt*.[136] These sayings are nevertheless just as true as the things that correspond to them are real. Even the duality which splits up the Book of God into an Old and a New Testament is relative to men: *Semel locutus est Deus, duo haec audivi*: both express fundamentally the same Christ; but this Christ, the incarnate Word, is a real being, really prepared for in history, and in Him God really expresses His own nature to men in its entirety.[137] The result is that, however relative the multiplicity of the words of Scripture may be, as so many biblical facts, or acts of the Logos, or again as so many phenomena of this Cosmos which is, so to speak, His first revelation, nothing in all this is illusory or vain. It is all objective, it is all grounded in being and plays its part in a real process. With more truth than in Buddhism it can be affirmed that the Logos does not lie. It would be impossible, in fact, to imagine a maxim such as this of Candrakirti's transposed into Christian terms: "Emptiness is the one refuge from all beliefs, but you must not believe in emptiness."[138] Nor can one imagine any Christian equivalent of the doctrine held by certain highly logical sects, according to which it is necessary to reject the whole of the Buddha's teaching if one wishes to attain one's ultimate deliverance.[139] "When a man has reached the other bank, what does he do with the boat? Does he carry it on his back, or does he abandon it?"

(iv) The "Buddha Land"

Here, to conclude, is our final comparison. As to hear the Buddha properly, so to see him properly and share in his "Land" it is necessary to be considerably advanced in perfection.[140] But this is not to say that this "Land" is "in itself" any different from ours or any of the intermediary "lands".

A simple extract may help us to understand this better than any abstract explanation, by revealing the idealism and relativism that dominate Mahayanist theory. The following story, which is taken from the *Vimalakirti nirdana sutra*, is intended as a reply to the naive question: Where is the Land of Buddha?

"When a Bodhisattva", said the Buddha, "wishes to gain access into a pure Land, he must purify his mind: as soon as this is purified, his future Land of Buddha is purified too."

On hearing these words, Sariputra thought secretly to himself the following objection: "If it is true that when the Bodhisattva is pure in mind his world is pure too, how is it that our Land of Buddha should be so impure when the Buddha established it by means of his pure mind when he was a Bodhisattva?"

But the Buddha, divining Sariputra's thoughts, questioned him thus: "Sariputra, is it the fault of the sun and the moon if the blind cannot see their light?"

"No, Master, it is not the fault of the sun and moon, it is the fault of the blind."

"Sariputra, it is therefore not the fault of the Tathagata if the creatures are prevented by their evil deeds from being able to see the purity of our Land of Buddha. In truth, Sariputra, this Land is always pure: it is you who cannot see its purity."[141]

Sankhasuda thereupon intervened and said to Sariputra: "O Sariputra, do not imagine that this Land of Buddha is not pure. For in my eyes the world established by the Blessed Sakyamuni is pure and without spot, as pure as the palaces of the Vasavartin gods."

And Sariputra replied: "In my eyes, this world is full of hills, mountains, hollows and holes, dust, grit, rocks and many other unpleasant, impure things."[142]

Sankhasuda replied: "The unevennesses and impurities are in your own mind."

At that moment the Buddha touched the ground with the tip of his foot and immediately the whole three thousand of the chiliocosms appeared, decked out in myriads of priceless jewels, like to the Buddhas' Lands of precious stones, whose virtues are limitless. And all the Hearers in the assembly found that they were sitting on a lotus of precious stones.[143]

Eastern Christianity has preserved in its mystical tradition ways of thought not very far removed from that which underlies this story.[144] Some people may recognise a kind of family likeness between this conversation and a certain dialogue which took place one winter morning at the beginning of the nineteenth century on the edge of a forest. The speakers there were not Sakyamuni, Sariputra and Sankhasuda, but St. Seraphim of Sarov and Motovilov, one of his disciples.

"My friend," said the saint, "we are both at this moment in the Mind of God. Why will you not look at me?"

"I cannot look at you, my Father," I replied. "Your eyes flash lightnings, your face has become more dazzling than the sun and it hurts my eyes to look at you."

"Have no fear," he said, "at this moment you have become as bright as I. You too are present in the fullness of the Mind of God; otherwise you would not be able to see me as you do."[145]

Every reality, every "land" is a representation, and every representation is relative to the condition of the person contemplating it.[146] We here find ourselves once again faced with the idea which Origen expressed when commenting on the *transfiguratus est ante eos* of the Gospels. And so we may say that in the Eastern mystical tradition too we come across a doctrine of generalised transfiguration. This is the doctrine elaborated by Gregory Palamas and recently brought to our attention again by Lossky. According to Palamas, in fact, "during His earthly life, Christ always shone with all the brightness of the divine light, which to the majority remained invisible. The Transfiguration was not an event circumscribed in time and space: no change took place in Christ at that moment, even in His human nature, but there was a change in the consciousness of the apostles, who for a short space of time were given the faculty of seeing their Master as He was, shining in all the brightness of the eternal light of His divinity".[147] Exactly as it was in the case of the Buddha, when he "touched the ground with the tip of his foot" so that Sariputra and Sankhasuda should see him for a moment in all his glory.

I do not wish to suggest that Gregory Palamas's explanation of the Transfiguration involves any profound debasement of Christianity;[148] particularly as it could be supported by other passages from Christian antiquity besides the no doubt risky speculations of Origen. We may read, for instance, in the *Book of the Mysteries* by St. Maximus the Confessor, that Christ "said to the good thief: 'Today thou shalt be with Me in paradise'; then, as what is to us the earth is for Him in no wise different from paradise, He appeared again on this earth and talked with His disciples".[149] This and other Patristic texts seem to suggest the same idea. Although devoid of any real Docetism, they would, if carried too far, lead one to believe that behind the appearance of a man existing under ordinary conditions Christ was already, for anyone with a sufficiently penetrating eye, shining in all the glory of divinity. From this point of view the miracle that took place on the mountain would not perhaps consist so much in the Transfiguration itself as in all the other moments of the earthly life of Christ; or rather, if there was any miracle at that moment, it would lie rather in the power of supernatural perception granted for one brief moment to the three disciples, without any real change needing to take place in Christ Himself. In normal times, in the eyes of fleshly men, *videbatur ut homo*; as a marvellous privilege, three men were called to contemplate Him as He always was, *in Dei gloria*.[150] No doubt St. Ambrose, when he used these expressions in his splendid letter to Ambrosius Sabinus, had no intention of introducing any speculations on this miracle; still less, of denying or toning down, however slightly, the *vera hominis forma*[151] in Christ; on the contrary, his whole idea was to prove this, with all the reality which it involves of Christ's redemptive activity.[152] Nor, indeed has Gregory Palamas any intention of denying it either, although his theory, which is much more emphatic, and much more one-sided, sets us on the dangerous slope that leads down to Docetism.[153]

As for the account of St. Seraphim of Sarov, and other similar accounts, they need cause us less anxiety. In fact, it is quite clear that these miraculous phenomena are intended to suggest an anticipation of the world to come. This, in fact, has been explicitly stated. Behr-Sigel says, for example: "By causing the transfiguration of man and the whole of nature to take place *hic et nunc*, through the gift of the Holy Spirit, the saintliness of St. Seraphim communicates a feeling of the closeness of the Kingdom of God; announcing the resurrection of the dead and the life of the world to come."[154] There is here an eschatological perspective which has no equivalent in Buddhism.

Certainly one must be suspicious of any attitude from which the universe tends to be regarded as nothing more than one vast illusion: such an attitude would be a remarkable betrayal of Christianity, annihilating its very substance and making it simply one aspect, only superficially different from any other, of an amorphous mysticism of the Void. This kind of mysticism always has a powerful attraction for a certain type of mind; it is one form of the danger which comes to us from India. However, if we keep the thought of the Four Last Things firmly in mind, then, once the act has been performed which decides each person's destiny, the idealist explanation takes on some of its rights again. And it is indeed to be met with in a more or less modified form in the most orthodox tradition of Western Christianity as well as in that of the East. Consider, for instance, as regards its heavenly aspect, this passage from Newman:

We think heaven must be a place of happiness to us, if we do but get there; but the great probability is, if we can judge by what goes on here below, that a bad man, if brought to heaven, would not know he was in heaven;—I do not go to the further question, whether, on the contrary, the very fact of his being in heaven with all his unholiness upon him, would not be a literal torment to him, and light up the fires of hell within him. This indeed would be a most dreadful way of finding out where he was. But let us suppose the lighter case: let us suppose he could remain in heaven unblasted, yet it would seem that at least he would not know that he was there. He would see nothing wonderful there.[155]

And here is Simone Weil taking a symbol from the Greeks she loved:

Ulysses, who had been carried away during his sleep by strangers, woke in a strange land, longing for Ithaca with a longing that rent his soul. Suddenly Athena opened his eyes and he saw that he was in Ithaca. In the same way every man who longs indefatigably for his country, who is distracted from his desire neither by Calypso nor by the Sirens, will one day suddenly find that he is there.[156]

We are here far from any Mahayanist theory. Anyone who longs for a country is not living in a world of illusion, he does not wish for something that he already possesses: on the contrary, it is his longing (provided that it has been roused and purified by the gift from on high) which takes him there.

A similar idea governs Origen's speculations on the divine Fire—the "consuming Fire" mentioned in Scripture,[157] the Fire of Love "refracted into anger by sin",[158] the Fire which sees and judges, intolerable to those whose imperfections it consumes or whose ill-will it burns away, whilst others it enlightens and inflames with love, assimilating them to itself.[159] Within their own narrower limits the Latin theologians of the Middle Ages, too, explained how the same fire of hell produces very different effects according to the kind of beings it touches.[160] But here again the resemblance to Buddhism is only partial and distant. Forgetting the atmosphere of magic in which the idealism of the Great Vehicle so often appears,[161] let us restrict ourselves to the principle behind it. It not only affects all the heavens and hells; it extends to every domain, to every level of reality, and eats them away: "the total destruction of the two views of existence and non-existence—such is the true character of things preached by the Buddhas."[162]

"This world," says "The Lotus of the Good Law,"[163] "is not created nor does it die; it does not travel through samsara nor does it get out of it." And the *Prajnaparamita* says: "Although the Bodhisattva leads an infinite number of creatures into nirvana, in reality there are neither any Bodhisattvas to do the leading, nor any creatures to be led."[164] And Asanga, the interpreter of all the great Mahayanists, from the Madhyamika to the Vignanavada, says: "In reality there is no difference between production and extinction, between samsara and nirvana."[165] This is the theme of the "nirvana which cannot be entered" and the "nirvana which is not the final stop";[166] of the mutual impregnation of the Tathata and the Sunyata, a theme taken up endlessly by all the learned writers of the School, for whom "this Triple World is entirely made up of thought (sittamatra)", and ending "in that identification of contraries which in the East is the last word on religious truth".[167] It returns everywhere with a persistence and monotony which would drive us to despair, and can calm only those who imagine that they have no longer any need of hope, or rather those who have been awakened out of "illusion" but have not yet "awakened" to hope, and have not learnt from God Himself to taste its pure savour. "Salvation," concludes Asanga, "is the destruction of a simple prejudice, and no one is saved."[168] According to Christianity, on the other hand, there is a real mystery of "the New Man". Everything cannot be reduced in this way to an awakening of consciousness or return to consciousness which is denied as soon as done. When such awakenings and returns occur, then, in so far as they are experienced, they do no more than represent—or anticipate through grace, and always in hope—certain changes of a more profound nature, whose significance is truly ontological, and which are themselves conditioned, as we said earlier, by one genuine, profound Intervention, an Intervention culminating in the Sacrifice of the Incarnate Saviour. In other words, conversion, "metanoia", is not a purely intellectual thing: it is an act, an effective movement from one state to another, demanding a personal decision, a personal adherence, an effective "Yes", as a result of which what happens afterwards is really different from what happened before. It is not sufficient for salvation simply to become conscious that one is already saved: one needs to be delivered from an evil which is only too real, and triumph over a death which is only too real. That is why the principle of our salvation is not to be found in one privileged moment of enlightenment, Bodhi; the redemption of the world will come as the result of the Act which is consummated upon the Cross.[169]

NOTES

[1] Quoted by O. Oldenberg, "Le Bouddha". English trans. by W. Hoey, 1882. Cf. the remark made by Sakyamuni to some parents crying for their child: "Whatever you love only brings you trouble and pain."

[2] Cf. Asoka, 1st Edict (on rock), 7th Edict (on a pillar). (*Les Inscriptions d'Asoka*, translated with a commentary by Jules Bloch, Collection Emile Sénart, 1950, pp. 91 and 172.) This respect for life seems, moreover, not to be the result of any feeling of pity but rather of the "desire to remain pure from the stain of the world". Cf. Albert Schweitzer, *Les grands penseurs de l'Inde*, Fr. trans., p. 73. For the rest, in ancient Buddhism the monks had no scruples about eating meat or fish, provided that "the animals were not sacrificed before their eyes or exclusively for themselves". A. Foucher, *La vie du Bouddha d'après les textes et les monuments de l'Inde*, p. 249; cf. p. 306.

[3] For ahimsa, cf. Paul Oltramare, *La théosophie bouddhique*, p. 51.

[4] *Der Buddhismus*, p. 170.

[5] Cf. the "Stances de Dharmika Subhuti", 105: "In everything, to act simply with a view to the good of others and to abstain from whatever does them harm—that is good behaviour." (Ed. Paul Mus, *La lumière sur les six voies*, 1939, p. 293.)

[6] From *mitra* (friend).

[7] *Itivuttaka*, 27. Compare the hymn to Charity in 1 Cor. xiii.

[8] "Relation de la compilation du Tripitaka," in J. Przyluski, *Le Concile de Rajagrha*, p. 102.

[9] *Majjhima-Nikaya*, I.

[10] R. P. Allo, *Plaies d'Europe et baumes du Gange*, p. 183. Cf. P. Oltramare, *op. cit.*, p. 522.

[11] *Dhammapada*.

[12] A Chinese Buddhist story in the collection made by Edouard Chavannes, *Cinq cents contes et apologues*, vol. I, p. 32.

[13] A legend of the Sarvastivadins, summarised by Louis de La Vallée-Poussin, *La morale bouddhique*, p. 213; see also p. 209. *Avadanasataka*, IV, 6.

[14] *Majjhima-Nikaya*, I.

[15] Cf. J. Hackin, *Collections bouddhiques du Musée Guimet*, pp. 80–81.

[16] Cf. Louis de La Vallée-Poussin, *op. cit.*, p. 85.

[17] Quoted by N. Soderblom, *Manuel d'histoire des religions*, Fr. trans., p. 297.

[18] This interpretation is fairly common. For example, one reads in Karl Adam's *Le Christ notre frère*, Fr. trans., p. 115: "As for Buddhist 'benevolence', it is something purely negative—the absence of any ill-feeling against one's neighbour."

[19] Cf. Paul Oltramare, *op. cit.*, pp. 138–139.

[20] Nagarjuna, *Mahaprajnaparamitasastra*, I, ch. XXI (trans. E. Lamotte, vol. I, p. 783).

[21] *Op. cit.*, p. 106.

[22] Louis de La Vallée-Poussin, *op. cit.*, p. 223.

[23] The full story is related in the *Kalpanamanditika*, the *Avadanakalpalata*, the *Lankavatara*. Nagarjuna quotes it and comments on it, *op. cit.*, ch. VIII (Lamotte, vol. I, pp. 255–260). The *Jatakamala* simply speaks of a "gift of eyes".

[24] It is to be found, either as a painting or a sculpture, at Mathura, Amaravati, Ajanta, in the Gandhara, in Central Asia, at Barabudur, etc. Cf. Alfred Foucher, "Les Représentations des Jataka dans les anciennes écoles indiennes", in *Mémoires concernant l'Asie orientale*, vol. III (1919), pp. 17–18.

[25] Cf. René Grousset, *Sur les traces du Buddha*, pp. 102 and 141. See, *ibid.*, the stories of the wild duck (p. 161), and the good hare (pp. 146–147, after the *Jataka*, 316, and *Caruya Pitaka*, I, 10; trans. in Chaine-Grousset, *Littérature religieuse*, pp. 711–712). As is well known, the story of "the pound of flesh" supplied Shakespeare with the plot of *The Merchant of Venice*.

[26] Already honoured in the Hinayana, at least by those at its centre. The *Mahavagga*, VIII, 26, quotes Sakyamuni's saying: "Whoever wants to take care of me must take care of the sick", as the conclusion to one of its moral fables. And the *Vinaya Pitaka*, I, 302: "O monks, you no longer have any mother or father to look after you. If you do not look after each other, who will take

care of you? Whoever, O monks, wants to take care of me, must look after the sick."

27 Cf. Jean Filliozat, in *Journal asiatique*, June 1934, p. 303. A similar phenomenon takes place in the West in the evolution of monasticism: cf. Stephan D'Irsay, *Histoire des Universités . . .*, vol. I, p. 102.

28 Edicts on rock, 2, 4, 5, 8, 9; Edicts on pillars, 5, 7. Cf. *Les Inscriptions d'Asoka*, translated with a commentary by Jules Bloch (Collection Emile Sénart, 1950).

29 René Grousset, *op. cit.*, pp. 121–122. The portraits given by Huian Tsang, and, following him, by Grousset, are undoubtedly idealised. See the remarks made by Paul Mus in the *Bulletin de l'Ecole française d'Extrême-Orient*, vol. XXXIV, p. 236.

30 Trans. Burnouf, p. 205; p. 8 (verses written by Maitreya).

31 Trans. Chavannes, in *Cinq cents contes et apologues*, vol. I, pp. 2–3. "Thus did the heir to the throne, the Prince Sie-ta-na (Sudana), who showed generosity towards the poor as a father nourishes his children, and who, when driven from his home by his father the king, felt pity but not hatred."

32 According to legend, when the future Buddha was born as the Prince Visvantara, "when he came forth from his mother's womb, he stretched out his right hand and said: 'Isn't there anything in the house, Mother? I wish to give alms'."

33 Ch. IX, n. 17 (trans. Lamotte, p. 248). For gradations within dana: Santideva, *Bodhicaryavatara*, VII, v. 25. Cf. Asoka, 11th Edict on rock: "There is no gift like the gift of the Law" (Bloch), p. 119.

34 Trans. Przyluski, *Le Concile de Rajaghra* (1931), p. 102.

35 Léon Feer, *Fragments traduits du Kandjour* (1883), p. 18.

36 Cf. Jean Przyluski, *La Légende de l'empereur Açoka* (1923), p. 255.

37 *Mahavagga*, I, 11 (ed. Oldenberg, 1879, p. 12). Cf. the legend of Purna: "Go, Purna; having been delivered yourself, deliver others; having been consoled, console others; having arrived at absolute nirvana, help others to get there" (in Burnouf, *Introduction à l'étude du Buddhisme indien*, p. 253).

38 Commentary on the *Bodhicaryavatara-panjika*.

39 Cf. Solange Bernard, "Le Bouddhisme", in Chaine-Grousset, *Littérature religieuse*, pp. 677–711. A very significant passage in the *Majjhima-Nikaya* (I, 38), about the monk "washed by the inner

washing": "He comes forward, having drenched the four quarters of a heart possessing love, compassion, joy, equilibrium; above, below, across, everywhere, he goes forward with a heart that is large, vast, limitless, bearing no hostility or ill-will, and which has drenched the world everywhere, for the benefit of all categories of being . . ." (Cf. Coomaraswamy-Horner, *Living Thoughts of Gotama the Buddha* (Living Thoughts Library), Cassell, 1948.

⁴⁰ G. Tucci, *Forme dello spirito asiatico* (1940). Cf. *Bibliographie bouddhique*, 1949, n. 625.

⁴¹ Lesson V, 11 (trans. E. Sénart, pp. 92–93).

⁴² It is in the Pali Canon that the story of the good-hearted hare is to be found, along with many others. For illustrations of this *Jataka* in the art of Ceylon, both painting and sculpture, cf. F. Taymans d'Epernon, *Les paradoxes du Bouddhisme* (1948), p. 33.

⁴³ Nagarjuna, *op. cit.*, ch. XXVIII (Lamotte, vol. I, p. 984).

⁴⁴ Trans. J. Bacot, p. 285.

⁴⁵ Cf. René Grousset, *Sur les traces du Bouddha*, an English edition of which was published by Cassell in 1932 under the title *In the Footsteps of the Buddha*. See also *Bilan de l'histoire*, pp. 153 and 160–164.

⁴⁶ Cf. Philippe Stern, "De l'amour humain à l'amour mystique dans les fresques d'Ajanta" (*L'amour de l'art*, a special number about India, 1947, pp. 291–300): "Here, we feel, is the incarnation of the essence of Buddhism" (p. 298).

⁴⁷ *Abhidharmakosa*, ch. III, n. 93, 94 (trans. La Vallée-Poussin, vol. III, p. 192), a description of the Buddhas of charity. (It is not absolutely certain that this Vasubandhu is the brother of Asanga.) Cf. *Ekottara*, IV, 1, etc.

⁴⁸ *Mahayanasutralamkara*, ch. XIII, 20, 22 (S. Lévi, p. 158), etc. Cf. ch. XVII, 33–68 (pp. 214–224); ch. XIX, 65 (p. 282).

⁴⁹ *Bodhicaryavatara*, ch. VIII. Cf. Origen, *In Ezechielem*, Homily I, n. 1, on the compassionate "descent" of the higher angels. See Jean Daniélou, *Origène*, pp. 244–245.

⁵⁰ Santideva, *op. cit.*, ch. V, v. 109 (Finot, p. 68). Cf. the verse quoted by Nagarjuna, *op. cit.*, ch. VIII:

> *Those skilful in the Mahayana*
> *Have compassion on all,*
> *They give their head and their eyes*
> *And sacrifice them for a bundle of straw.*

[51] Santideva, *op. cit.*, ch. VII, v. 51 (Finot, p. 96). For the fight against pride: *ibid.*, vv. 56–59 (pp. 96–97).

[52] See again Santideva, *Siksasamuccaya*, ed. C. Bendall (1902), p. 196.

[53] *Sutta-Nipata*, vv. 149–150.

[54] *Siksasamuccaya* (Bendall, p. 212). Cf. Nagarjuna, *op. cit.*, ch. XX: "To all beings the Bodhisattva gives with perfect equanimity; he gives without seeking any reward and (thus) realises the true character of giving" (trans. Lamotte, vol. I, p. 709). Milarepa, the last words of advice to the *Repas*: "Those who are full of worldly desires can do nothing for others. They do not even do anything that profits themselves. It is like a man carried away by the current trying to save others" (trans. Jacques Bacot, "Le poète tibétain Milarépa", p. 284).

[55] Spinoza, *Ethica*, I, v. prop. 19: *Qui Deum amat, conari non potest, ut Deus ipsum contra amet.* Léon Brunschvicg, *Le Progrès de la conscience* . . . vol. II. A penetrating criticism of this "generosity" will be found in Pierre Lachièze-Rey, *Le Moi, le Monde et Dieu*, new ed. (1950), pp. 127–132.

[56] vv. 90–91, 113–114 (Finot, pp. 113 and 116), etc.

[57] *Jatakamala*, I, 17 (quoted by P. Oltramare, *Théosophie bouddhique*, p. 105, n. 1). To understand the full meaning of this method, which is not simply a method, cf. *infra*. See also the passage from Milarepa quoted by J. Bacot, *op. cit.*, p. 286: "The interest of others is achieved by identifying oneself with others."

[58] *Le Lotus de la Bonne Loi*, note to ch. I, p. 300.

[59] *Journal des Débats*, 4th April 1853.

[60] Cf. Henri Bernard, in the *Revue apologétique*, December 1933.

[61] Taine's point of view can be found discussed by F. Pillon in the *Année philosophique*, 2nd year (1868), especially pp. 413–414.

[62] 5th January 1881: "The abolition of desire and the practice of charity comprise the Buddha's whole method, the whole art of deliverance."

[63] *Philosophie analytique de l'histoire*, vol. II (1897), p. 147; cf. pp. 124 and 154.

[64] "La loi d'amour et la loi de justice", in the *Critique philosophique*, 1873, vol. I, p. 212.

[65] Léon de Rosny, *Le Bouddhisme éclectique* (1894), p. 170. Similarly L. de Milloué, *Le Bouddhisme dans le monde* (1893), pp. 111–115.

[66] R. Pischel, *Leben und Lehre des Buddha* (4th ed., 1926).

[67] *Le Mythe du héros et la mentalité primitive* (1932), p. 28. "St. Martin only gives half his cloak; he keeps the other half for himself, and it is a man who benefits from his generosity. The Buddhist sage immolates himself completely, and it is an animal which profits from his supreme sacrifice. Here we have the difference between the beliefs of the West, which are always moderate and sensible, and those of the East, which take the noblest tendencies of the human soul to absurd lengths. Nevertheless the principle that dominates all these stories, Biblical, Christian or Buddhist, remains the same: they are all performances, dramatisations of moral and religious beliefs." *Ibid.* Cf. Tetsujiro Inone, "La situation du bouddhisme dans le monde spirituel" (*Bulletin de la Maison franco-japonaise*, vol. VIII, 1937, p. 78): "Buddhist pity is wider than Christian love . . . it extends to all living beings."

[68] A. Foucher, in *Revue de l'histoire des religions*, vol. CLVI (1902), pp. 90–91, a summary of Oldenberg, *Aus Indien und Iran* (1899). In his recent *Vie du Bouddha* (p. 27), Foucher is less dogmatic.

[69] Which for him excludes justice and makes "civil society" impossible.

[70] *La théosophie bouddhique*, p. 412.

[71] Renouvier has noted these "childish elements" from which the "miraculous fantasy of Buddhist charity" is woven: *Philosophie analytique de l'histoire*, vol. II, p. 201.

[72] Renan, *Nouvelles études d'histoire religieuse*, p. 86.

[73] A. Foucher, *La Vie du Bouddha*, p. 75.

[74] These characteristics are summarised by Renan, *op. cit.*, p. 166. A similar story is told in the *Mahavastu* and in the *Lalitavistara*: Sakyamuni accepts a bowl from each of the four "great Kings" of space and makes one bowl out of the four, thus disappointing none of them.

[75] *Tchrimakundan*, translated by Jacques Bacot in *Trois mystères tibétains* (1921). Cf. the introduction by Bacot, pp. 23–24. An English edition, trans. H. I. Woolf, was published in 1923 under the title *Three Tibetan Mystery Plays*.

[76] This story is described by R. Grousset, *Sur les traces du Bouddha*, pp. 99–100.

[77] *Op. cit.*, p. 412. The same may be said of another *Jataka*. When he was a prince, the Bodhisattva met a tigress which was dying of hunger with its little ones; immediately he wished to be devoured by it, but the tigress lacked the strength to eat him; he then gashed himself, the blood flowed, and by licking the blood the tigress recovered enough strength to eat him.

[78] Visvantara's attitude may be compared with that of Makar Ivanovitch, in *The Adolescent* by Dostoievsky. Makar Ivanovitch gets rid of his wife as casually as he would dispose of an old piece of clothing, in order to advance towards perfection. On this Jacques Madaule comments as follows—his remarks apply equally here: "Our Western conscience is shocked by a husband who gives his wife away, even though he does not sell her. Dostoievsky ... did not understand that, just as the Church is incarnate here below ... so this miserable world of the flesh is not entirely devoid of value. ... The end of Dostoievsky's vision was a kind of Christian anarchy; a complete neglect of rights and duties and a contempt for that minimum of law without which no society is conceivable." *Le christianisme de Dostoiewski*, p. 176.

[79] *Op. cit.*, p. 108.

[80] Cf. Asanga, *Mahayanasutralamkara*, ch. XVI, 16 (trans. Sylvain Lévi, p. 182): "An insatiable tendency, an enormous tendency, a joyous tendency, an obliging tendency, an uninhibited tendency, a tendency towards the Good ... the Bodhisattva would like at every moment to create World Levels as numerous as the sands of the Ganges, all filled with jewels, so as to be able to give them away. ... The sons of the Buddhas have at all times sacrificed their lives for the first beggar who came along, out of pure compassion, without asking anything in return," etc. See also N. Péri, in the *Bulletin de l'Ecole française d'Extrême Orient* (1911), p. 443.

[81] Another practice which costs little is giving one's corpse in advance to dogs or birds. In Tibet they sometimes even manage to get it eaten by men. Cf. René Follet, *Les sommets de la pensée indienne*, p. 81.

[82] Nagarjuna, *Mahaprajnaparamitasastra* ("Traité de la grande vertu de sagesse"), I, ch. XX (trans. E. Lamotte, vol. II, p. 721).

[83] Or else, in certain cases, the "ecstasies of charity" are carefully regimented, as for instance those under Harsa, which so surprised Huian Tsang. There was a certain ceremony called the pancarsa,

attributed by tradition to the Emperor Asoka, during which large amounts of money were given away. Harsa, along with other kings, celebrated this festival every five years, always in the same way. And the vassal princes were able to buy back, probably at purely token prices, treasure which had been distributed to the clergy. Cf. Paul Mus, *Bulletin de l'Ecole française d'Extrême Orient*, vol. XXIV, fasc. 1, p. 236.

[84] Santideva, *Bodhicaryavatara*, ch. V, v. 10 (Finot, p. 53). Louis de la Vallée-Poussin, *Etudes et Matériaux*, pp. 108 and 117. Paul Oltramare, *op. cit.*, pp. 328–329 and 398–399. There then takes place a kind of indeterminate reaction in both directions, and this is what Jean Thamar calls a "kind of circular rhythm of cosmic charity": "Prajnaparamita", in *Etudes asiatiques* (Zürich, 1949), p. 21. Cf. the rite of the "burning of the head" in the ceremony of incorporation into the sangha: through the nine little tonsures which are made on the head by nine sticks of burning incense, the recipient is supposed to immolate himself for the salvation of beings. The principle behind such a symbolism is quite legitimate and very fine—provided it is made effective in act.

[85] Vasubandhu, *Karmasiddhiprakarana* (trans. E. Lamotte, *Mélanges chinois et bouddhiques*, vol. IV, 1935–1936, p. 263).

[86] There are many such passages (Vasumitra, Vasubandhu, Asanga, etc.). Cf. *supra*, n. 49.

[87] Vasubandhu, *Abhidharmakosa*, III, p. 10: "Although no new beings appear, and although innumerable Buddhas enable innumerable beings to attain to nirvana, the beings of the innumerable universes will never be exhausted."

[88] When the great Bodhisattva Avalokita entered into it, the burning heat changed immediately to delicious coolness, and in place of the cauldron in which the damned were boiling there appeared a beautiful calm pool covered with lotus flowers. Cf. Glasenapp, *Brahma et Bouddha*, Fr. trans., p. 214.

[89] *Journal de voyage d'un philosophe*, Fr. trans., vol. I, pp. 48–49 and 61. These pages, so literary in their tone and so tainted with a polemical spirit, are particularly concerned with the doctrine of the Little Vehicle. Christianity also teaches one "to mistrust an all-devouring activism which leaves no time for loving" (Joseph Folliet, in his report to the Congrès de l'Union des Oeuvres, Lyons, April 1950). But though Buddhism avoids the indiscretions of such an

activism—from which our Western zeal is not always exempt—there is another side to it: it knows nothing of the violence of love.

[90] Pierre Charles, *Semaine sociale de Paris* (1928), p. 206.

[91] Nicolas Berdyaev has justly written: "At one time it was the fashion to reject compassion in favour of love . . . but this involved a profound error from the moral point of view. For though compassion is not the whole of Christian love, which knows incontestably higher levels, it cannot be excluded from it. But there is more to it than this: ethics itself could not exist without pity. In our fallen, sinful world, pity points more clearly than anything else to the existence of another world and to the memory which we have of it" (*De la destination de l'homme*, p. 250).

[92] Yves de Montcheuil, "Le ressentiment dans la vie morale et religieuse d'après Max Scheler", in *Mélanges théologiques* (1946), p. 200.

[93] Saint Augustine, *In epistulam Joannis ad Parthos*, tract. 8, n. 5 (P. L., 35, 2038–2039).

[94] Santideva, *Bodhicaryavatara*, ch. VIII, vv. 94, 101, 102 (Finot, pp. 113–114).

[95] Nagarjuna, *op. cit.*, I, ch. X: "The Bodhisattva knows that no Dharmas are either born or destroyed and are devoid of any nature of their own. If anyone hates him or insults him, strikes him or kills him, he looks upon all this as a dream, a metamorphosis" (trans. Lamotte, vol. I, p. 320).

[96] "Kumarajiva" (413), a summary by Léon Wieger, *Histoire des croyances religieuses et des opinions philosophiques en Chine*, 2nd ed. (1922), p. 427. "'But,' replies the objector, 'can it be called real pity when it is for beings envisaged in such an impersonal way?' 'Yes,' says Kumarajiva. 'For the P'ou-sa (Bodhisattva) really offers his pain and his merits, which are real.' However, one difficulty still remained: how to reconcile even this general and abstract kind of pity with the fourth degree of dhyana, which assumes unconsciousness? To this point Kumarajiva did not reply. A popular and very simple answer was to be found in stories of Buddhas and Bodhisattvas voluntarily leaving their quietude when they wanted to act and show pity on people, and returning to it when they wished to rest."

[97] Cf. J. Przyluski, *Le Bouddhisme* (1932), p. 33: "A fervour free from excessive sentimentality, analogous to Christian charity, for it has only definite beings as its object."

98 When the comparison is made with our common idea of pity the contrast is true. Thus, for instance, we read in Jacques Bacot, *Milarépa*, p. 25: "Our pity . . . is highly subjective. It aims at bringing comfort, and hiding certain kinds of suffering which we find too disturbing. It does not endeavour so much to prevent suffering as to prevent any expression of it. Punishments which we find too painful, for instance, have been abolished because they pain those who watch them. Buddhist pity has no connection with this kind of sentimentality. It is quite objective and cold, and based on a metaphysical conception. It is not spontaneous but comes at the end of a series of meditations. It is pity for all who live and are mis-led by illusion, and is generated by a kind of idealism which tends to identify the ego and the non-ego. It embraces all beings drawn by their passions into the cycle of rebirth. It is universal, whilst ours is particular."

99 Or one may say: the idea of a thing (dharma) has a higher reality than the thing itself in its subjective existence (sattva).

100 Cf. Paul Oltramare, *op. cit.*, pp. 152, 382–383, 469; L. de la Vallée-Poussin in *Mélanges chinois et bouddhiques*, I (1932), p. 70; Paul Mus, in *Bulletin* . . . (1928), p. 191. On the other hand, there is the concrete, universal pity of, for instance, Isaac of Nineveh; cf. *Les Paroles d'Isaac le Syrien* (Moscow, 1858, p. 299): "I was asked to explain what a heart full of pity is, and I replied: 'It is a human heart which embraces the whole creation—men, birds, animals, demons, and every kind of creature; when he thinks of them his eyes stream with tears, a great and poignant feeling of pity possesses him and his heart is gripped with intense suffering, and he cannot bear to see or hear any pain or sorrow endured by any creature; and so from hour to hour he prays in tears for all dumb creatures and for the enemies of truth and for those who harm him, that God may look after them and pardon them; and even for reptiles he prays with great pity—and this pity it is which elevates his heart im-measurably until it becomes assimilated to God.'" Vladimir Solo-viev, who quotes these words (*La justification du bien*, Fr. trans., 1939, p. 72), observes that it "is difficult to believe that such a naïve description could contain any artificial rhetoric or exaggerated pathos". Cf. E. Behr-Sigel, *Prière et sainteté dans l'Eglise russe* (1950), p. 115, who notes in St. Seraphin of Sarov "the classical qualities of the Russian staretz: his gentleness, his forgiveness of his enemies, and, above all, his infinite charity for all human suffering".

[101] Nagarjuna, *op. cit.*, ch. VIII (Lamotte, vol. I, p. 298) and ch. XX (p. 724).

[102] This is asserted by an expert in the Mahayana: "from the Buddhist point of view Christianity is Hinayanist, since it makes a rigorous distinction between man and God." Tetsujiro Inoue, "La situation du bouddhisme dans le monde spirituel", in *Bulletin de la Maison franco-japonaise*, vol. VIII (1937), p. 76.

[103] "In Thee, my God, I will have my solidity, my fixity, my definite being" (St. Augustine).

[104] St. Paul, 1 Cor. xiii. 13. Cf. Evagrius Ponticus, Letter 56 (fragm. 605; P. G., 40, 1382): "The first commandment is charity; it is by this that the soul is drawn towards the Supreme Charity, which is God."

[105] Cf. Paul Claudel, *Sur la Présence de Dieu* (1932), p. 23: "As the Buddhists have clearly seen, we can go down into the very depths of ourselves, down all the rungs of introspection, without meeting anything but a fluid, volatile, endlessly changing element—the movement which proceeds from potentiality to act—until we grasp being itself, that active image of God within us which is our substance, cause, our spirit and our life, and which is known in the Holy Books essentially as *firmamentum*. God, says the Book of Kings, has been made my firmament."

[106] Quoted, with reference to another point of doctrine, by Stcherbatsky, *The Conception of Buddhist Nirvana* (1927), p. 50.

[107] Max Scheler, *Nature et formes de la sympathie* (trans. Lefebvre, p. 121). Contrast the ideal of the Christian monk as described by St. Athanasius in his *Life of St. Anthony*: "When his solitude bears its fruit, it becomes clear that it is the fruit of charity." Fr. Louis Bouyer, *La Vie de saint Antoine, essai sur la spiritualité du monachisme primitif* (1950), pp. 116–117.

[108] Granet, *La Religion des Chinois*, p. 167.

[109] Asanga, *Mahayanasutralamkara*, ch. XVI (S. Lévi, pp. 177–178). Cf. the *Sandhinirmocanasutra*, ch. IX, n. 9–11 (trans. E. Lamotte, pp. 243–245).

[110] *Cinq cents contes* . . ., vol. I, p. iii. Cf. "The Lotus of the Good Law", ch. I: "And after making these gifts, with calm minds they demand the knowledge of the Tathagatas" (trans. Burnouf, p. 7).

[111] According to Taranatha this was also to have been the order in the work by Asvaghosa: a hundred of the Buddha's earlier existences were to have been described in this work, each ten corresponding to one of the paramitas.

[112] "Prajnaparamita", in *Etudes asiatiques* (Zürich, 1949), p. 22, and in *Etudes traditionnelles* (1950), p. 171.

[113] Candrakirti, "*Madhyamikaratara*"; cf. P. Oltramare, *op. cit.*, pp. 407–411.

[114] Nagarjuna, *op. cit.*, ch. I (Lamotte, pp. 1 and 14–15): ch. XVIII and XIX (pp. 658–659 and 666 *et seq.*). Sometimes Nagarjuna expresses the two states of mind here mentioned by one word: Mahamaitrikarunasitta (p. 52).

[115] Nagarjuna, *op. cit.*, ch. XIV (Lamotte, vol. I, p. 480); cf. ch. XV, p. 559.

[116] Léonce de Grandmaison, "Les religions de l'Inde", 5th lesson (*Bulletin de la Conférence Saint-Michel*, March 14th, 1926, p. 21): "It should be noted that the Buddha's last life contains none of these miracles of piety. . . . Good works of this kind have brought him to the end, have made his Karma perfect. But in the last stage, detachment and asceticism appear alone, bringing Deliverance beyond good and evil, transcending any attachment to either of these."

[117] This is explained, again by Asanga, *op. cit.*, ch. IX, 28–33: "As the world is illumined by the brightness of the sun's rays, which are all thrown out at once, so the whole realm of the comprehensible is illumined at once by the knowledge of the Buddhas" (S. Lévi, p. 77; cf. 18–19 (p. 74)).

[118] "Les trois corps du Buddha", in *Journal asiatique*, May–June 1913, pp. 589–590.

[119] We must think here not only of Spinozism but of every doctrine—and is there any exception to be found, outside the sphere of influence of the Christian or Jewish faiths?—which does not dare to assert God's absolute independence of His creation. For instance, there is this poem by Rabindranath Tagore:

Thou hast taken upon thyself the chains of creation . . .
O Lord, master of all the heavens, if I did not exist where would be thy love?
Through my life thy will takes shape endlessly . . .

And that is why, King of Kings, thou hast clothed thyself
with beauty to capture my heart . . .

Thou givest thyself to me through love and then in me thou
becomest aware of thy perfect sweetness.

[120] Ch. VI, vv. 116 and 118 (Filot, p. 84).

[121] Cf. Origen, *In Ezechielem*, Homily VI, n. 6 (Klostermann,
pp. 384–385). See *Histoire et Esprit, l'intelligence de l'Ecriture d'après
Origène*, pp. 241–243. See also P. Lachièze-Rey, *op. cit.*, pp. 136–138.

[122] For St. Anthony, the father of monasticism, cf. Louis Bouyer,
op. cit., pp. 66 and 155–156.

[123] *Mahavagga* (trans. E. H. Brewster, *Gotama le Bouddha*, p. 82).

[124] This account is not peculiar to the Pali Canon. See, for
example, the Tibetan version in the translation by Léon Feer,
Fragments extraits du Kandjour, pp. 22 and 26: there is the same grading
in the Buddha's first speech to Yasa, and the same silence about
charity in the second, in which Sakyamuni gives "a complete
exposition of the Law, developing it as it really is".

[125] *Catuhsataka*, ch. VIII, n. 189 (trans. P. L. Vaidya, p. 131).

[126] Nagarjuna, *op. cit.*, ch. XXX (Lamotte, vol. I, p. 1083).

[127] Cf. Henri de Lubac, "Le commentaire d'Origène sur
Jérémie", XX, 7, in *Mémorial Joseph Chaine* (Lyon, Facultés
catholiques, 1950), pp. 255–280.

[128] The classic comparison: cf. Paul Demiéville, art. "Byo", in
Hobogirin (1937), fasc. 3, p. 232*b*; and E. Lamotte, *Notes bouddhiques*,
Académie Royale de Belgique (1935), p. 301.

[129] Cf. Louis de La Vallée-Poussin, *Etudes et matériaux . . .*, pp.
78 and 116; and *Muscon*, vol. XI (1910), p. 278. In the possession
of absolute truth there is no moral progress, any more than there
is any "intellectual progress"; it is believed that all Dharmas,
whatever they may be, "are to be neither admitted nor rejected,
all being a kind of magic, a dream, an optical illusion, an echo,
the moon in the water, a ghost" (Candrakirti). Here we cannot
define this technical idea of the Void (Sunya) any more closely;
it often approximates to that of relativity.

[130] Part One, ch. XIV (Lamotte, vol. I, p. 470). "It is only
when united with the Prajnaparamita that it is called a Paramita
and leads to the state of Buddhahood."

[131] Ch. XX and XXI. There is a similar tendency in Eastern Christianity. See, for example, St. Maximus the Confessor, *Exposition of the Our Father* (P. G., 90, 888 A); *On Charity*, IV, 41–44 and 86 (P. G., 90, 1029 A–B and 1069 A–B); *Ambigua* (P. G., 91, 1249 A–B); cf. Hans Urs von Balthasar, *Liturgie cosmique*, pp. 242, 254, 263, 265. M. Lot-Borodine, in the *Revue de l'histoire des religions*, vol. CVI, p. 571. I. Hausherr, in *Orientalia christiana periodica* (1935), p. 138: "Brotherly love was looked upon as above all a means to personal perfection, a necessary medicine against the irascible passions which were regarded as the greatest obstacle to the life of prayer. It is for this reason that charity manifests itself above all as gentleness and a resolution always to forgive others." However, cf. *supra*, note 100.

[132] Ch. IX, vv. 1–3 and 75–77 (Finot, pp. 128 and 138–139).

[133] Ch. IX, vv. 150 and 155 (Finot, pp. 150 and 151). The tenth and last chapter refers again to dana. But in this chapter there is no advance on chapter IX. It is "a parinamana, an 'application' of the author's 'merit'—and the author does not flatter himself that he possesses Prajna, except possibly a few grains of it. When the Perfection of Wisdom has been reached, one is above any idea of difference, one is a Buddha." Louis de la Vallée-Poussin, in *Revue de l'histoire des religions*, vol. LVII (1908), p. 347, note 1. It is highly significant that in the study which he devoted to "La carrière du Saint bouddhique" (*Bulletin de la Maison franco-japonaise*, vol. II, 1929, pp. 1–22), a work which is based on the sources, Jean Rahder was unable to make any categorical statement about any kind of charity.

[134] Cf. the Abbé Paul de Broglie, *Problèmes et conclusions de l'histoire des religions* (1886), p. 200: Christianity is as far above Buddhism "as a real living body is above a ghost".

[135] Philippe Stern, *loc. cit.*, p. 298. See also Germain Bazin, who quotes this passage from Stern: "Le visage de miséricorde", in *Le Coeur*, Etudes Carmélitaines (1950), p. 331. Bazin reminds us that Grousset (following Victor Goloubew) compared the "fine Bodhisattva" at Ajanta to Leonardo da Vinci's figure of Christ in the Last Supper (and particularly to Leonardo's study for this Christ, now at Brera). There is the same "rather tired, forward stoop", the same "ineffable gentle sadness", the same "look of commiseration for the human condition". But it is worth noting that the word "dream" comes spontaneously to his mind: "These representations of the supernatural at Ajanta are amongst the most

moving that have ever entered human dreams." Meanwhile, is it quite certain that Leonardo da Vinci's work "breathes the pure spirit of the Gospels" (Eugène Muntz, *Léonard de Vinci*, 1899, p. 185), and that "if ever any picture of Christ could approach our idea of Him", it would be this picture at Brera? (Cf. René Grousset, *Bilan de l'histoire*, pp. 131 and 162.)

[136] Traces of this misunderstanding will be found in the book by Tetsujiro Inoue, from which we have quoted, *loc. cit.*, p. 77.

[137] To which his friend Charles Secrétan replied that in the authentic Christian idea, "there is no justice without love, nor is there any love without justice; the love-feeling is not love. Love is the will that there should be being" (March 17th, 1869), *Correspondance de Renouvier et de Secrétan*, p. 19. See also *Proudhon et le christianisme* (1946), ch. IV, published in English by Sheed and Ward under the title, *The Un-Marxian Socialist*.

[138] Cf. the definition given by de la Vallée-Poussin, "Maitri et Arana", in *Société belge d'études orientales* (1921), p. 91: "A sort of affectionateness or abstract friendship with which the monk envelops all beings in all four directions."

[139] René Grousset, *Bilan de l'histoire*, p. 128. Obviously, it would be a mistake to stress the comparison between pre-Buddhist India and pre-Columbus America.

[140] *Idem*; Introduction to the volume of art, *De l'Inde au Cambodge et à Java* (the text is by Jeannine Auboyer) (1950), p. xii.

[141] It may be said of this, what Albert Schweitzer says of ethics in general: "It is a dangerous enemy that Buddha introduces into the fortified enclosure of the negation of the world" (*Les grands penseurs de l'Inde*, p. 105). But the dangerous enemy has been firmly tied up.

[142] *Sunyatasunyata*, the eighteenth and last kind of sunyata (emptiness) distinguished by the Madhyamika School. Cf. P.-L. Vaidya, *Etudes sur Aryadeva* (1923), p. 41.

[143] "Mahamudra des Sutra", a Tibetan work of the seventeenth century, translated by Jacques Bacot, *Le Bouddhisme* (1940), pp. 102–104. Cf. *Prajnaparamita Hridaya sutra*, translated by Jean Thamar, *loc. cit.*, p. 12: "O Sariputra, in this world, form is Void and the Void is form; form is nothing but the Void and the Void is nothing but form; where there is form there is the Void, where there is the Void, there is form. The same is true of sensations, thoughts, acts of will

and consciousness ... O Sariputra, in this world all things have the nature of the Void; they are not born, nor do they die away; they are neither pure nor impure; they neither increase nor diminish." What René Grousset says of Candrakirti may be said of many others: he "is intoxicated with emptiness" (*Les Philosophies indiennes*, 1931, vol. I, p. 319).

144 Sakyamuni's words after his enlightenment. Cf. Nagarjuna, *op. cit.*, I, ch. X: "This profound law means Emptiness, the not-taken-into-consideration and the characterless" (Lamotte, vol. I, p. 338). In practice the doctrine of the Void in the Mahayana takes the place of the phenomenalism of the doctrine of impermanence in the Hinayana.

CHAPTER II

1 Cf. Gilbert Combaz, "L'évolution du Stupa en Asie", in *Mélanges chinois et bouddhiques* (1935–1936), vol. IV, pp. 109 and 114–115. Ananda K. Coomaraswamy, *Elements of Buddhist Iconography* (1935), fig. 1.

2 Which destroys the following assertion by Foucher: "No one will be surprised to find that ancient Buddhist art centres entirely round the legend of the Master. It goes without saying that, in their search for subjects, artists turned directly to scenes in which morality was shown in action: abstract rules and metaphysical speculations hardly lend themselves to the purposes of illustration." In a note, Foucher simply says: "An exception must be made of the famous wheel at Ajanta." ("Scènes figurées de la légende du Buddha", in *Etudes de critique et d'histoire*, 2nd series, 1896, p. 102.) In fact Buddhists always showed themselves highly ingenious, from the very first period of their art, in giving their speculations (which, incidentally, it hardly seems right to describe as "metaphysical") artistic form.

3 Cf. Charles Martin, "Un περὶ τοῦ πάσχα de saint Hippolyte retrouvé"? in *Recherches de science religieuse* (1926), pp. 148–165; "Fragments palimpsestes d'un discours sur la Pâque attribué à saint Hippolyte de Rome", in *Mélanges Franz Cumont* (1937), vol. I, pp. 321–363; "Hippolyte de Rome et Proclus de Constantinople", in *Revue d'histoire ecclésiastique* (1937), pp. 255–276. The author intends to study the suggested attribution more fully. A manuscript of the eighth or ninth century, which has been preserved in the Abbey at Grottaferrata, contains the first third of the Homily

(with a number of variants of archaic character), and attributes it expressly to Hippolytus under the title Εἰς τὸ ἅγιον πάσχα. See, at present: *Homélies pascales, I, une homélie inspirée du traité sur la Pâque d'Hippolyte*, studied, edited and translated by Pierre Nautin (Coll. *Sources Chrétiennes*, 1950).

[4] *Sixth Homily on Easter* (P. G., 59, cols. 743–746; Nautin, 51, pp. 176–179). The sentence begins with the neuter gender and ends with the masculine. Similarly, in n. 62, the author, like St. Paul, equates Christ with Easter (p. 189).

[5] The famous Sarnath Pillar is certainly a cosmic pillar too. But is it Buddhist? Cf. *infra*.

[6] "The Lotus", ch. I, v. 67.

[7] VI, 30 and 62 *et seq.* The *Mahavamsa* is a Singhalese Chronicle.

[8] Sylvian Lévi, *Le Népal*, vol. II, p. 4. Paul Mus, *Cultes indiens et indigènes au Champa* (Hanoi, 1934); *Barabudur, esquisse d'une histoire du bouddhisme fondée sur la critique archéologique des textes: Journal asiatique*, vol. CCXXVIII (December 1936), an account by Coomaraswamy, "Elements . . ."

[9] Cf. Henri Focillon, *L'Art bouddhique* (1921), pp. 33–34: "A stupa was originally a tumulus erected around relics of the body of the Buddha, which had been divided up after his death and carefully preserved in caskets and vases . . . Indian symbolism compares it to an air bubble floating on the top of the waves, an image of the vanities of earthly life. A pious tale shows the Buddha deciding how it was to look and teaching his disciples how it was to be honoured: taking three cloaks and folding them into four, he put his upturned begging-bowl on top of them and on top of the bowl he put his itinerant monk's stick. From this simple formula the whole of the architecture of Buddhist Asia has gradually grown up."

[10] Cf. Mme. Odette Viennot, "L'arbre dans l'iconographie bouddhique" (a typewritten memoir, 1946, Bibliothèque du Musée Guimet). For the tree of Buddha-Gaya: *Dipavamsa*, 15; *Mahavamsa*, 18–19. In the "Lotus" and the *Lalitavistara*, the Buddha and the tree appear more than once inseparably joined together.

[11] Ch. XVI (trans. Burnouf).

[12] Ch. V, n. 29–33.

[13] Cf. Kramrich, *Indian Sculpture* (1933), n. 209. Coomaraswamy, *op. cit.*, figs. 4, 5 and 6.

[14] *Theragatha*, n. 1095.

[15] *Dhammapada*, n. 387.

[16] Cf. the description by Huian Tsang, in his reminiscences (trans. as *Mémoires* by St. Julien, vol. I, pp. 459–462).

[17] V. 29–40: "They saw three men emerge from the tomb: two of them were supporting the third, and a cross followed them. And the heads of the first two reached to the sky, but the head of the one they were leading went beyond the heavens."

[18] N. 90 and 91 (Christ at the Transfiguration): "And His head touched the sky"; 93: "He appeared to me sometimes like a giant whose head touched the sky."

[19] *Similitude* 9, ch. VI, n. 1: "I saw a multitude advancing; in the middle was a man whose height was so colossal that He overlooked the tower." (This is the Son of God, who seems to have been for Hermas the first of the Seven Wise Men mentioned in Scripture.)

[20] Lucius Charinus, *Apostolorum Periodi* (a summary of the *Acts* of Peter, John, Andrew, Thomas and Paul), quoted by Photius, *Bibliotheca*, cod. 114 (P. G., 103, 390 C). The *Acts* of SS. Perpetua and Felicity, c. 4 and 10. *Madracha* of St. Ephraem, 4th Sunday after Whitsun: "He was lying in the tomb like a weak creature, and today He has risen like a giant"; an allusion to Ps. xviii, 5–6, found earlier in St. Justin, "Dialogue with the Jew Tryphon", c. 64, n. 8, and in St. Irenaeus, *Adversus Haereses*, l. IV, c. 33, n. 13 (P. G., 7, 1082 A). The Elcesaites also made Christ a giant: Hippolytus, *Philosophumena*, l. IX, c. 3, n. 13. St. Augustine, *Contra sermonem arian.*, 8 (P. L., 42, 689). Leporius, *Libellus emendationis*, 6 (P. L., 31, 275 D). Cf. *IV Esdras*, II, 43: "Juvenis statura celsus eminentior omnibus illis."

[21] St. Ambrose, *De incarnatione*, l. V, c. 35 (P. L., 16, 827 C).

[22] Cf. Strack-Billerbeck, III, 851; IV, 888, 946. See also *Poimandres*, 1: "It seemed to me that there appeared before me a being of immense size, great beyond all measure" (Nock-Festugière, p. 7; cf. the references, p. 8, note 3).

[23] Cf. Arturo Graf, *Miti, leggende e superstizioni del Medio Evo* (Turin, 1925), pp. 59–65 and p. 126.

[24] *Speculum Ecclesiae, De inventione sanctae crucis* (P. L., 172, 944). Details in W. Meyer, *Die Geschichte des Kreuzholzes vor Christus* (Münich, 1881).

[25] "Un poète regarde la croix." He gives the following explanation as "read somewhere": "For the Cross was not made of just any kind of wood. A bough was first taken from the tree of good and evil and planted over the tomb of the first man. This branch developed and grew so magnificent that no other tree could be compared to it. This was the predestined tree, the mysterious, imperishable trunk. It was one of the branches of this tree that the dove brought to Noe in the Ark. Later, another supplied Moses with the rod with which he struck the rock. It went to the making of the bridge over the torrent which Solomon suggested to the Queen of Sheba, and on which, out of respect, she refused to step when she entered Jerusalem. It was then miraculously preserved at the bottom of the Pool of Probatica until the time of the Passion" (p. 52).

[26] "In the middle of the town and on both banks of the river there was a tree of life . . . whose leaves were for the healing of the nations." St. Justin, 1st *Apology*, c. 55. Origen, *Contra Celsum*, VI, 34. Pseudo-Ambrose, *Sermon 45*, 3: "Sicut per arborem mortui, ita per arborem vivificati; arbor nobis nuditatem ostendit, arbor indulgentiae foliis vestivit" (P. L., 17, 692), etc. Cf. R. Bauerreis, *Arbor Vitae, Der 'Lebensbaum' und seine Verwendung in Liturgie, Kunst und Brauchtum des Abendlandes* (Münich, 1938). H. Bergema, *The Tree of Life in Scripture and in History* (in Dutch, 1938): an account is to be found in the *Revue d'histoire ecclésiastique* (1939).

[27] *Tractatus II*. Cf. the *Opusculum III* of St. Bonaventure: "Lignum Vitae", etc.

[28] Cf. Fr. Congar, "Jésus-Christ Agneau de Dieu", in *Foi et Vie* (1947), p. 56: "I am persuaded that [this cross] is to be interpreted in this way, as an artistic representation of Christianity itself."

[29] Haseloff, in A. Michel, *Histoire de l'art*, vol. II, i, p. 346. L. Walk, quoted by Mircea Eliade, *Traité d'histoire des religions*, p. 283. Cf. H. Leclercq, *Dict. d'archéologie chrétienne et de liturgie*, "Arbres" (vol. I, cols. 2706–2707); "Baptistère" (vol. II, cols. 406–407); "Pontien" (vol. XIV, cols. 1415–1416). In the blessing of fonts, the form prescribed for the breathing on the water is reminiscent of the form of the Tree of Life.

[30] "Emmaus", p. 66.

[31] See also "Canon sancti Patris Theodori Studitae in adorationem crucis", Oda prima: "Appareto, o immensa Domini crux,

ostende mihi nunc divinam faciem venustatis tuae (*Ἐπιφάνηθι ὁ μέγας τοῦ Κυρίου σταυρός, δειξόν μοι ὄψιν θείαν τῆς ὡραιότητός σου νῦν*), in J. Gretser, S. J., *De sancta cruce* (Ratisbon, 1734), p. 321. Cf. P. Didrom, *Histoire de Dieu* (1843), p. 351: "The Cross is more than a figure of Christ; in iconography it is Christ Himself or His symbol ..."

[32] *In Psalmum I* (Pitra, *Analecta sacra*, vol. II, p. 445): ξύλον ὁ χριστος ἀναγέγραπται ἐν τῇ θεοπνεῦστῳ γραφῇ.

[33] *De Hominis Opificio*, c. XIX.

[34] *Contra Adversarium legis et prophetarum*, l. I, c. 15, n. 25–26: "Hodie mecum eris in paradiso.—Esse autem ibi cum Christo, hoc est esse cum vitae ligno. Ipse est quippe Sapientia, de qua ... scriptum est: lignum vitae est amplectentibus eum (P. L., 42, 616).

[35] *In Apocalypsim*, l. II (Maxima Bibliotheca Veterum Patrum, Lyons, 1677, pp. 434 H and 435 A–D); l. V (p. 509 C); l. X (p. 646 D). *Homilia in Transfiguratione Domini*, n. 12 (P. L., 89, 1312 C).

[36] *De divisione naturae*, l. V, c. 36: "Lignum vitae, hoc est Dominus noster Jesus Christus" (P. L., 122, 981 A); c. 38: "Vocatur Christus, quippe omnium bonorum lignum est fructiferum", etc. (1015 A).

[37] *De Trinitate et operibus ejus* (P. L., 167, 274–275); *In Cantica*, l. IV (P. L., 168, 895 D) and l. VII (953 D).

[38] *Expositio in psalmos selectos*, Ps. 1, 3 (P. L., 172, 277 B); *In Annuntiatione sanctae Mariae* (P. L., 172, 902 D). Cf. *De Claustro animae*, l. IV, c. 35: "Est etiam arbor vitae Christus in medio Ecclesiae (P. L., 176, 1173 C–D). Pseudo-Tauler, *Meditations on the Life and Passions of Jesus Christ*, ch. XXXVIII.

[39] "Le cerf et le serpent ..." in *Cahiers archéologiques*, IV (1949), pp. 17–60; p. 22: "The Chrism, the Cross, the Tree of Life ... would thus seem to be symbols of the same reality—Christ, the principle of the regeneration effected by the sacraments" (pp. 23–24). "Like the 'Water of Life', or the 'Living Water', the Bread of the Eucharist—the 'Bread of Life' or the 'Living Bread'—was commonly held to be the fruit of the 'arbor vitae', or the Cross, or —what comes to the same thing—the actual substance of the Body of Christ" (p. 55).

[40] *Congrès archéologiques de France*, session at Puy (1904), pp. 447–453. W. L. Hildebruch, "A Medieval Brass Pectoral Cross", in *Art Bulletin*, vol. XIV (1932), pp. 79–102. For the tree placed

between Alpha and Omega, the symbol of Christ: *Dictionnaire d'archéologie chrétienne et de liturgie*, vol. I, col. 2697. See again Hippolytus, *In Prov.*: Καρπὸς δικαιοσύνης καί δενδρον ξωῆς, ὁ χριστος ἔστὶν (P.G., 10, 620 D).

These examples of Christian crosses may be compared with the grass crosses made in Nepal for the Indra-Yatra. During the week of this festival, held in honour of Indra (August–September), crosses are to be seen everywhere, absolutely covered with leaves or grass, and on them appear the head, hands and feet of the god. The crosses are venerated, but they are also pierced with arrows: this rite is supposed to attract the life-giving rain. Indra, who is identified with the cross, is the god of rainy skies, which stretch throughout space in all directions. Cf. Sylvain Lévi, *Le Népal*, vol. I, p. 53; Pierre Saintyves, "Le culte de la croix dans le bouddhisme, en Chine, au Népal et au Thibet," in *Rev. de l'hist. des rel.* (1917); and the curious book by Fr. Augustin-Antoine Georgi, of the Hermits of St. Augustine, quoted by Saintyves: "Alphabetum Tibetanum, Missionum Apostolicarum commodo editum; praemissa est disquisitio qua de vario litterarum ac regionum nomine, gentis origine, moribus, superstitione ac manichaeismo fuse disseritur, Beausobrii calumniae in sanctum Augustinum aliosque Ecclesiae Patres refutantur" (Rome, 1772).

[41] James of Sarugh, *Homily on the Vision of Jacob at Bethel*, n. 95 (Zingerle-Mosinger, *Monumenta Syriaca*, vol. I, Œniponte, 1869, p. 26). Cf. Isaac of Antioch (G. C. Bickel, *S. Isaaci Antiocheni . . . opera omnia*, vol. I, Giessae, 1873, p. 90). Passages quoted and translated by Carl-Martin Edsman, *Baptism of Fire* (Leipzig-Upsala, 1940), pp. 51–53. Aphraates, *Homily on Prayer*: "The ladder which Jacob saw is the mystery of our Saviour, by whom men ascend from the bottom towards the top; it is also the mystery of the Cross of our Saviour, which was raised like a ladder and at whose summit stood the Saviour" (Patr. Syr., vol. I, p. 146).

[42] *Tu nos hinc per modum scalae*
Ducas ad caelestia.

(Blume-Bannister, *Thesauri Hymnologici Prosarium*, vol. II, Leipzig, 1922, p. 20.)

[43] This bridge has three parts, corresponding to the three stages in the spiritual ascent: the feet, sides and mouth of Christ. This passage and others, with comments from a different point of view, will be found in Père Louis Beirnaert's "Le symbolisme ascensionnel

dans la liturgie et la mystique chrétiennes", in *Eranos-Jahrbuch*, vol. XVIII (1950).

[44] St. Augustine, *In psalmum CXIX*, n. 1 (P. L., 37, 1597). The tiered pillar in the Buddhist stupas, symbolising Mount Meru, corresponds to both the ladder and the mountain mentioned in Christian texts.

[45] "Hymn XI", 11 (T.-J. Lamy, *Ephraem Syrus, Hymni et Sermones*, 1883, vol. I, col. 95). The passage from our Pseudo-Hippolytus too says, concerning the tree of the Cross: "It is Jacob's ladder and the way of the angels, and at the top of it the Lord is truly to be found" (Nautin, 51, p. 176).

[46] The same phrase occurs in a manuscript: ὁ Ἰησοῦς; and in another: στύλος πυρός. Lipsius-Bonnet, *Acta Apostolorum Apocrypha* (1903), vol. II, 2, p. 10, and the note.

[47] P. Lecau, *Fragments d'apocryphes coptes* (Cairo, 1904), p. 76.

[48] "Quomodo prior potero orare, cum tu sis columna luminis?" Dom André Wilmart, *Analecta Reginiensia* (Studi e Testi, LIX, 1933), p. 333, n. 12. Cf. Wilmart-Tisserant, "Fragments grecs et latins de l'Evangile de Barthélémy", in *Revue biblique* (1913), pp. 349 and 354.

[49] A. Wallis Budge, *Coptic Apocrypha in the Dialect of Upper Egypt* (London, 1913), pp. 271-272. "The Life of Bishop Pisentius", by John the Elder, fols. 32-33: "It is said concerning the holy man Apa Pisentius, that it came to pass on a time when he was young, while he was pasturing his father's sheep, that God opened his eyes, and he saw a pillar of fire in front of him. Now there were certain other young men who were pasturing sheep with him. And he said unto the other young men who were pasturing sheep with him: 'Do ye see the pillar of fire on the road in front of us?' And they said unto him: 'We do not see it.' Then he cried out up to heaven, saying: 'O God, open then the eyes of these young men, so that they may see the pillar of fire even as I see it.' And God hearkened unto his voice, and the eyes of the young men were opened, and they saw the pillar of fire. And observe ye now, O my beloved, that the moment when God chose Moses was when He spoke unto him in his early manhood, out of a pillar of fire [which went up] out of a bush."

[50] See again Amélineau, *Etudes sur le christianisme en Egypte au VIIe siècle* (1887), pp. 5-8 and 74-75.

[51] F. C. Burkitt, *Early Eastern Christianity* (London, 1904), pp. 43–44: C. R. C. Allberry, *A Manichaean Psalm-book* (Stuttgart, 1938), vol. II, p. 139.

[52] H. Odeberg, *III Enoch, or the Hebrew Book of Enoch* (Cambridge, 1928), p. 123. For these different passages on the Ladder and the Pillar see the book already quoted by C. M. Edsman, pp. 48–56 and 158–172.

[53] *De errore . . .*, c. XXI, n. 4–5 and c. XXVII, n. 3. Ed. G. Heuten (1938), pp. 97 and 99.

[54] First *Apology*, c. LX.

[55] *In Marcum XV* (its authenticity is not absolutely certain), *In Ezechielem* (P. L., 25, 423 B).

[56] St. Augustine, *In psalmum XCV*, n. 15 (P. L., 37, 1236).

[57] St. Maximus of Turin, *Homilia L* (P. L., 57, 342).

[58] *First Homily on the Exaltation of the Cross* (P. G., 97, 1021 C).

[59] Amalarius, *De ecclesiasticis officiis*, l. I, c. 14 (P. L., 105, 1031 D); *De ordine antiphonarii*, c. 33 (P. L., 105, 1285 D). Rabanus Maurus, *De laudibus sanctae crucis*, twelfth figure (P. L., 107, 195–198 and 277). Othloh of St. Emmeram, *Dialogus de tribus quaestionibus*, c. 39 (P. L., 146, 113 C–D). Honorius of Autun, *Gemma animae*, l. III, c. 42 (P. L., 172, 654–655); *Sacramentarium*, c. 4 (741); *Speculum Ecclesiae* (946); *Elucidarium*, l. I, c. 11 (1117). Sicard of Cremona, *Mitrale*, l. VI, c. 13 (P. L., 213, 214), etc. Once again, Paul Claudel's book may be referred to, "Un poète regarde la croix", pp. 149 and 244.

[60] Compare the Indian tradition which puts the centre of the world at an elevated spot (in the Himalaya district), whence flow, through four orifices shaped like the head of an animal, four rivers (Sita, Ganges, Indus and Oxus) towards the four points of the compass. Cf. J. Przyluski, *La Grande Déesse* (1950), pp. 66–67.

[61] Which put the centre of the world at the rock of the Temple in Jerusalem.

[62] See, for example, St. Ambrose, *In Lucam*, l. X, n. 114: "Ipse autem crucis locum, vel in medio, ut conspicuus omnibus, vel supra Adae, ut Hebraei disputant, sepulturam" (P. L., 15, 1832 C).

[63] Florus, "Carmen XX", in *Monumenta Germaniae Historica, Poetae latini aevi carolini*, vol. II, p. 548 (cf. Dom Ceillier, vol. XII, pp. 490–491). Cf. St. Jerome, *Epist. XLVI* (ed. Hilberg, vol.

I, p. 332). Origen, *In Matthaeum* (P. G., 13, 1777). Rabanus Maurus, *Ad Praeclarum episcopum* (M. G. H., *Poetae latini . . .*, vol. II, p. 179), etc. Perhaps the fact that the sun and moon are shown on each side of the Cross has a similar significance.

64 Office of the Exaltation of the Cross, *La prière des Eglises de rite byzantin* (Mercenier-Paris), vol. II, Part I, pp. 39 and 52.

65 Mme. Odette Viennot, *op. cit.*, p. 133. Cf. *Jataka Bhaddasala*, n. 485.

66 *Op. cit.*, p. 49. Cf. W. Burlingame, *Buddhist Legends from Dhammapada*, Pali text (Harvard Oriental Series, 1929), A. K. Coomaraswamy, *Yaksa*, vol. II, pl. 25, 3.

67 *Op. cit.*, p. 50. For the Buddha and the River Nairanjana, cf. J. P. Vogel, *Indian Serpent Lore* (1926), pp. 97–102. Emile Sénart, *Essai sur la légende du Buddha* (1882), p. 349: "There is nothing more common in Buddhist legend than the appearance of Vanadevatas, spirits which preside over trees and make their homes in them." *Ibid.*, p. 205, another similarity with Vedic mythology.

68 *Mahavamsa*, I, 52–57. Cf. O. Viennot, *op. cit.*, p. 43.

69 *Lalitavistara*, ch. XXI. Cf. O. Viennot, *op. cit.*, p. 42.

70 E. W. Hopkins, "Mythological Aspects of Trees and Mountains in the Great Epic", in *Journal of the American Oriental Society*, vol. XXX (1910), pp. 348–349: "This is mentioned several times, yet not as a tree in itself undying, but as conferring deathlessness, aksayakarana, or as making endless the offering there given to the Manes."

71 O. Viennot, *op. cit.*, pp. 40–41 and p. 46. Cunningham, *The Stupa of Bharhut*, pl. xv. M. Ramaprasad Chanda, *Beginnings of Art in Eastern India*, n. 30, p. 5. E. Sénart, *op. cit.*, p. 355: "The reason for the respect shown to the tree . . . lies in the fact that it is identified with the god himself; this idea . . . will help one to understand the close connection between the tree and the Bodhisattva in the supreme conflict which decides his mission, in the legend about his birth according to which he did in fact come out of the tree. In his struggle with the Buddha, Mara directs his efforts as much as and even more against the tree than against the saint himself."

72 *Rig-Veda*, I, 24, 7; IV, 13, 5; V. 29, 4; X, 82, 5; X, 89, 4. *Atharva-Veda*, X, 4, 3; X, 7, 38. *Chandogya Upanishad*, VI, 8, 4; VI, 11, 1; VI, 12, 2. *Maitri Upanishad*, VI, 1–4; VI, 35; VII, 11. *Svastasvatara Upanishad*, III, 9. *Taittvya Upanishad*, I, 10.

[73] *Katha Upanishad*, VI, 1.

[74] *Maitri Upanishad*, VI, 4; etc. It will be noticed that the two titles refer both to Bodhi and to the Buddha.

[75] *Rig-Veda*, I, 59.

[76] Trans. Louis Renou, *"Hymnes et prières du Veda"* (1938), pp. 127–131.

[77] Cf. the Indian book of the *Trente-deux récits du Trône*, trans. L. Feer, pp. 127–128: "At the top of Mount Udaya there is an altar to a god, and in front of this an unseen lake from which on four sides descend staircases made of shining gold, ornamented with precious stones, pearls and coral. In the middle of the lake is a column of gold, and on the column a throne decorated with all manner of jewels. Between the rising of the sun and the middle of the day the column gradually rises, bearing the throne upwards until it touches the face of the sun, from the middle of the day to the setting of the sun it gradually comes down again until it is back in the middle of the lake, as it was at the beginning. This happens every day." Quoted by Jean Przyluski, *La Grande Déesse* (1950), p. 68.

[78] Cf. M. S. Paranavitana, *The Stupa in Ceylon*, quoted by G. Combaz, *loc. cit.*, p. 54.

[79] *Rig-Veda*, III, 8, 3.

[80] *Maitri Upanishad*, VI, 6. In the *Rig-Veda* (X, 90) this was the part played by the Purusha, which "covers the earth and stretches beyond it".

[81] Later the same cosmic symbolism was to be expressed by a process in the opposite direction—not by a few signs, vaguely or symbolically human, added to a tree or a pillar, but by cosmic signs represented on a human body. In her book, *Le Trône et son symbolisme dans l'Inde ancienne* (1949, p. 149), Mlle. Jeannine Auboyer describes a statue of the Buddha in the Musée Guimet (No. MA 25): on the shoulders are the sun and the moon; on the chest Mount Meru; on the thighs the various kinds of Paradise; on the ankles the various hells. Similar figures have been discovered in Chinese Turkestan.

[82] Paul Mus, in *Journal asiatique*, vol. CCXXVIII (December 1936), p. 633.

[83] See the Rabbinical texts quoted by J. Bonsirven, *Exégèse rabbinique et exégèse paulinienne*, p. 237. In other writings (*IV Esdras*,

VIII, 52; *Test. David*, V) the Tree of Life was the future Jerusalem, the Messianic community: cf. L. Cerfaux, *La théologie de l'Eglise suivant saint Paul*, p. 277. Cf. *supra*, notes 33 to 38.

[84] Hermas, *The Shepherd*, Similitude VIII, 3. The Clementine writings also mention the "Eternal Law" which appeared to Moses and the Prophets.

[85] Origen, *On Prayer*, c. XXVII, n. 10; *In Joannem*, vol. XX, 36; *In Psalmum I*, 1 (P. G., 12, 1085 A); *In Rom.*, l. V, n. 9 (P. G., 14, 1043 C). *In Jesu Nave*, Homily VIII, n. 6: "Et magis fortasse, ut adhuc excelsius amplitudinem mysterii dilatemus, in hoc ligno intelligitur esse 'scientia boni et mali', in quo et bonus Christus et diabolus malus pependit . . . Sed haec tropice dici intelligenda sunt; Christus enim ipse dicitur 'arbor vitae'."

[86] Daniel, iv, 7–13.

[87] Jean Steinmann, *Daniel* (1950), p. 78.

[88] Ezech., xxviii, 13–14; cf. xlvii, 1–12. Compare the poem translated by P. Dhorme, *Choix de textes religieux assyro-babyloniens* (1907), p. 99. Similarly, in the epic of Gilgamesh, the hero goes up into the mountain looking for his ancestor Um-Napishti, "who succeeded in rising into the assembly of the gods", to question him "about death and life"; here he is at the end of his final stage (Tablet IX, Column V):

> When he had walked a full day's journey he saw a light shining.
> He then saw a tree and went straight towards it.
> The fruit which it bears is made entirely of rubies,
> Its branches stretch out wide and hang down and are lovely to look at;
> Its blue foliage is lapis-lazuli;
> It bears fruit and its life is wonderful!

(Trans. G. Conteneau, *L'épopée de Gilgamesh, poème babylonien*, 1939, p. 126).

Various proofs that the sacred tree was looked upon as a tree of life and light have been collected by A. J. Wensick, *Tree and Bird as Cosmological Symbols in Western Asia* (Amsterdam, 1921). See also Hélène Danthine, *Le Palmier-dattier et les arbres sacrés dans l'iconographie de l'Asie occidentale ancienne* (Paris, 1937), 2 vols. (text with plates): p. 153: "Sometimes garlands of palm-leaves surround the composition."

[89] Apoc., xxii, 1-2: "And he shewed me a river of water of life, clear as crystal, proceeding from the throne of God and of the Lamb. In the midst of the street thereof, and on both sides of the river, was the tree of life, bearing twelve fruits, yielding its fruits every month: and the leaves of the tree were for the healing of the nations."

[90] H. Danthine, *op. cit.*, p. 176 (and in the plates, figs. 955 and 956). Other Egyptian monuments represent a similar subject; corresponding texts speak of "the Lady of the Sycamore". Cf. L. Keimer, "Sur un bas-relief en calcaire représentant la déesse dans le sycomore et la déesse dans le dattier", in *Annales du service des antiquités de l'Egypte* (1929), vol. XXIX.

[91] Cf. Jean Przyluski, in *Mélanges Linossier*, vol. II, pp. 481-498; "Le symbolisme du pilier de Sarnath"; *Id.*, *La Grande Déesse* (1950), pp. 67-73.

[92] G. Combaz, *op. cit.*, p. 114. Goblet d'Alviella, "Le peigne liturgique de Saint-Loup", in *Croyances, rites, institutions* (1911), vol. I, p. 89. Compare the quotation *supra*, note 77.

[93] Jean Przyluski, *La Participation* (1940), p. 71. Cf. E. Sénart, *op. cit.*, pp. 350-351, on the high wooded mountain of Buddhist cosmology: "There are seven great lakes to which the Buddhas come and refresh themselves in baths which are entirely covered with wonderfully shining precious stones. By the side of the grotto of gems, the tree Manjushaka . . . bears every kind of flower that is to be found on sea or land . . . under its shade the Pratyekabuddhas engage in the exercise of the dhyanas. In this forest grows too the great Jambu, which rises to a height of a hundred yojanas; it covers an area of three hundred yojanas and divides into four branches which give birth to great rivers. During the whole kalpa of renovation it bears an immortal fruit that looks like gold."

[94] Jean Przyluski, *La Grande Déesse* (1950), p. 104.

[95] Odette Viennot, *op. cit.*, p. 20.

[96] For these examples and for others, see Mircea Eliade, *Traité d'histoire des religions* (1948), pp. 99-100, 232-260. G. van der Leeuw, *La religion dans son essence et dans ses manifestations*, Fr. trans. (1948), p. 47. M. Granet, *La Pensée chinoise*, p. 324. Uno Holmberg, "Der Baum des Lebens", in *Annales Academiae scientiarum Fennicae* (1922-1923), series B, vol. XVI. Cf. Tor Andrae, *Mahomet, sa vie et ses doctrines* (1945), Fr. trans., p. 11. "In Canaan, the sacred tree could be replaced by a stake, an *asera*."

[97] Marcel Granet, *La Pensée chinoise* (1934), p. 324. And is it not a fact that ancient China believed that the world had been made in the shape of a cross? *Op. cit.*, pp. 180 and 284–286.

[98] Mircea Eliade, *op. cit.*, p. 234: "The tree represents, either in a concrete, ritual way or in a cosmological, mythical way, or, again, in a purely symbolic way, the living Cosmos, endlessly regenerating itself. Endless life being equivalent to immortality, the Cosmos-tree can hence at another level become the tree of 'Life-without-death'. The same inexhaustible life being in the old ontology an expression of the idea of absolute reality, the tree then becomes the symbol of this reality (the centre of the world)". P. 237: "The idea of a 'centre', an absolute reality—absolute because it is a receptacle of the sacred—is implied in even the most elementary ideas of the 'sacred place', from which the sacred tree is never absent." Pp. 235–236: "One cannot properly speak of any 'worship of the tree'. No tree has ever been adored simply for itself, but always for what is revealed through it, what it implies and means. . . . By its mere presence ('power') and by its own law of evolution ('regeneration'), the tree repeats what in archaic experience *is* the entire Cosmos."

[99] For the tree of life at the centre of Paradise in the Rabbinical tradition, cf. in the *Yalkout Chimesui* (a collection compiled about the thirteenth century), a passage attributed to the Rabbi Josue ben Levi (third century): translated in A. Cohen, *Le Talmud*, Fr. trans. (1950), p. 457. A conception which is more profoundly cosmic, and not without a pantheistic tinge, will be found in one of the currents of Jewish mysticism. G. G. Scholem, *Les grands courants de la mystique juive*, Fr. trans. (1950), p. 230: "The ten Sephiroths (divine Powers) make up the mystic Tree . . .; each one represents a branch, and their common root is unknown and unknowable. But the En-Sof is not only the hidden Root of all Roots, it is also the sap of the tree; each branch, representing an attribute, does not exist by itself alone but in virtue of the En-Sof, the hidden God. And this Tree of God is also, so to speak, the skeleton of the universe: it grows throughout the whole creation and spreads its branches into all its endless ramifications. All the created things in the world only exist because of this: because something of the power of the Sephiroths is alive and active in them. "

Similarly, in Islam. The theology of Islam has the Quib, the axis or pole or centre of the universe. For some, this Quib, the divine Idea, the Word, the Spirit, is an aspect of Allah. It is known as "the first Angel", and on it turns the mill of created things (cf. the bhavacakra in Buddhism). It rules the heavens, the earth and hell. Ultimately the saint becomes the pole on which the universe turns. Cf. A. K. Coomaraswamy, *Elements of Buddhist Iconography*, n. 100.

[100] The form taken by the latter will seem less paradoxical if one accepts the idea towards which so many facts seem to tend: is it not from the sacred place, the centre and summit of the world, that stones and sacred trees are taken, retaining the properties of the sacred place? And, again, is it not "from the stele and the lopped tree that the statues of the divinities derive"? (Jean Przyluski, *La Grande Déesse*, p. 65; cf. J. Auboyer, *op. cit.*, pp. 52 and 60).

[101] A. K. Coomaraswamy, *op. cit.*, pp. 7–8. Cf. Emile Sénart, *op. cit.*, p. 207, referring to the *Lalitavistara*: the whole scene of the Buddha-Gaya is a "particular rendering of the myth of the gaining of ambrosia . . . nothing is more common than the assimilation of the fruit of the sambhodi to amrita". But the whole question is to know in each case what kind and degree of originality are involved in this "particular rendering".

[102] *Op. cit.*, n. 14. This syncretism—which is always tempting to iconographers—has found its fullest and most emphatic expression in another book by the same author recently translated into French (1949): *Hindouisme et Bouddhisme* (Coll. *Tradition*, vol. V). A similar illusion will be found in Titus Burckhardt, "Considérations sur l'alchimie" (*Etudes traditionelles*, 1949, pp. 120–123). One can see in this work the traditionalist spirit tainted with esotericism that crops up periodically and which produced, for instance, René Guénon's *Le Symbolisme de la Croix*.

[103] *L'arbre dans l'iconographie bouddhique*, pp. viii and 207.

[104] This even seems to be true for a detail like the gigantic stature attributed to Christ. In the *Evangile de Pierre*, p. 300, L. Vaganay sees this simply as a naïve invention made in all good faith to suggest either the sovereignty of the Son of God, or the glory of the One, without any suggestion of any heterodox origin. But if this feature is put alongside the other similar features mentioned earlier, it will hardly be doubted, it seems to me, that what we are faced with is some sort of original, mythical whole, which penetrated even into orthodox circles, by means of the Gnostics.

105 The revealed dogmas themselves, which in any case come into quite a different category from that with which we are concerned here, are not, in their formulation, affirmations which have simply "dropped from the sky" ready-made, so to speak. It is only a "curious myth" which sometimes attributes this idea to St. Thomas Aquinas, for instance. Cf. Victor White, O.P., "St. Thomas's Conception of Revelation", *Dominican Studies* (1948), vol. I, No. 1, pp. 1 ff. See also Jules Lebreton, S.J., in *Etudes*, (1907), vol. CXIII, p. 507, n. 1.

106 Cf. Colossians, i, 16–19.

107 N. 29, 54 and 63 (cf. Nautin, pp. 155, 181 and 191). The same idea occurs in Hippolytus, *Of Anti-Christ*, c. LXI: "Stretching His two holy hands out on the wood, Christ unfolded two wings, one to the left and one to the right, calling to Himself all believers and enfolding them as a hen protects its little ones" (Achelis, p. 42).

108 Everywhere there are to be found Christian documents concerning the symbolism of the cross which provide examples of this kind of transposition. Cf. Origen, *In Exodum*, Homily VI, n. 8: "magnitudinem brachii illius, quod Dominus expendit in cruce" (Baehrens, p. 199). Saint Jerome, *In Ezechielem* (P. L., 25, 423, B), etc. There is a double transposition, evoking on the one hand the universal Church and on the other the inner dimensions of the soul.

109 Here again, as in the old Indian symbolism, it can be said that "the throne in a certain sense surpasses the king": Jeannine Auboyer, *op. cit.*, pp. 189–190.

110 For in Buddhism it is much more a case of cutting the Cosmic Tree, the tree of all life, "at the root", than of drawing from it a renewal of a life of suffering. In Christianity the sensible forms of life are equally transcended, but the affirmation of Life triumphs: "In Him was life, and the life was the light of men" and "the darkness did not comprehend it." "I am the way, the truth and the life."

111 That is why it is in the end untrue to say that "non-anthropomorphic" portrayals of the Buddha, such as the stylised tree at Sanchi and the "Pillars of Fire" at Amaravati, are at the same time "personal" portraits. Cf. *supra*, n. 82.

112 The phrase is once again taken from our pseudo-Hippolytus, n. 55: ὁ κοσμικὸς ἀγών (Nautin, p. 181).

NOTE ON THE COMPARATIVE SYMBOLISM OF BUDDHIST AND CHRISTIAN PRIMITIVE ART

[1] A. Foucher, "Scènes figurées de la légende du Bouddha", in *Etudes de critique et d'histoire* (1896), 2nd series, p. 111.

[2] For these four main scenes in the life of the Buddha as portrayed in art: Vogel, *La sculpture de Mathura*, pp. 57–58.

[3] Nevertheless, on this eastern gate alone more than five hundred people are directly portrayed, not to mention the animals. On the rear front are to be seen seven empty thrones set under trees, for the seven successive Buddhas.

[4] Paul Mus, *Barabudur*, p. 65.

[5] See also R. Chanda, *Medieval Indian Sculpture in the British Museum* (London, 1936: cf. *Bibliographie bouddhique*, f. VII–VIII, No. 566). In his work, *Art bouddhique* (1921), p. 53, Henri Focillon simply says: ". . . This is not surprising when one thinks of the essence of the doctrine, then in the fullness of its purity, to which any personal cult, any idolatry of the founder, was repugnant."

[6] A. Foucher, *La Vie du Bouddha d'après les textes et les monuments de l'Inde* (1949).

[7] Cf. V. Goloubev, in *Bulletin de l'Ecole française d'Extrême Orient* (1923), pp. 449–454: "In short, the Greek influence, as transmitted through the forms used by the artists of Gandhara, is no more than a brief episode in the evolution of the Indian Buddha." J. Hackin, "Archéologie bouddhique", in *Revue des arts asiatiques* (1928), pp. 125–126. S. Kramrisch, *Indian Sculpture* (Coll. *The Heritage of India Series*, 1933), pp. 38–45 and 209–210. Phillippe Stern, "L'art de l'Inde", in L. Réau, *Histoire universelle des arts*, vol. IV, pp. 143–144. W. W. Tarn, *The Greeks in Bactria and India* (1938), pp. 393–408.

[8] Perhaps some indication might also be found in a canonical text, for according to Paul Demiéville, in *Hobogirin* (1937), fasc. 3, p. 210, art. "Butsuzo" (Image of the Buddha), "a passage from the Vinaya of the Saravastivadins, which indeed seems strangely out of place in its context, seems to preserve a trace of some original prohibition".

[9] Cf. Paul Mus, *Barabudur*, p. 60: "It seems inconsistent not to portray the Buddha . . . or to substitute for him a material sign, when he is one of many actors in an illustrated story."

[10] Paul Mus, *op. cit.*, p. 65.

[11] *Op. cit.*, p. 62.

[12] Cf. Jeannine Auboyer, *Le trône et son symbolisme dans l'Inde ancienne* (1949), p. 74.

[13] A. Foucher, *La porte orientale du Stupa de Sanchi*, Musée Guimet, popular library, (1910), vol. XXXIV, p. 177.

[14] *Barabudur*, p. 68.

[15] *Barabudur*, p. 66; cf. pp. 60–63.

[16] *Barabudur*, pp. 70–71. *La lumière sur les six voies* (1939), pp. vi–viii and p. xv.

[17] Jeannine Auboyer, *op. cit.*, pp. 188–189: "In India the symbolism of the throne, and all its sacred power, date from time immemorial; from the very earliest days of the holy place we find the throne identified with the altar and correlated with the other essential elements of the place, the tree-column and the water. The throne embodies all the characteristics which go to make up the cosmic synthesis . . . Standing at the centre of the world, it is correlated with the cosmic pillar; as such, it is closely associated with the myths of the Sun and the cakravartin. As the centre of the world it is immovable, the one stable point in the universal chaos, indestructible in its essence. It is a whole world in itself, like a mountain of gold, and the gods dwell on it."

[18] Paul Mus, "La mythologie primitive et la pensée de l'Inde", in *Bulletin de la Société française de philosophie* (1937), p. 91.

[19] It will be remembered that in the early stages of Buddhism "the Bhikshus were forbidden to loiter in places decorated with pictures": V. Goloubev, "Documents pour servir à l'histoire d'Ajanta" (*Ars asiatica*, x), p. 23. Was this merely for reasons of propriety?

[20] See, for example, Tatian, *Discourse to the Greeks*, or Minutius Felix, "Octavius", c. 29.

[21] Guillaume de Jerphanion, "La représentation de la croix et du crucifix aux origines de l'art chrétien", in the *Voix des Monuments*, vol. I, pp. 143–145 and p. 162. Max Sulzberger, "Le Symbole de la Croix et les Monogrammes de Jésus chez les premiers Chrétiens", in *Byzantion*, (1925), II, pp. 386–393. See also Dom H. Leclercq, in the *Dict. d'archéologie chrétienne et de liturgie* (1914), vol. III, art. "Croix".

[22] Cf. St. Paulinus of Nola, *Epist. XXXII*, describing the apse of his church: "The cross and the lamb signify the holy victim."

[23] M. Sulzberger, *loc. cit.*, p. 352, *Barnabé*, IX, 7–8.

[24] *Paedagogus*, l. III, c. 1.

[25] Cf. Hebrews, vi, 18–20.

[26] Tertullian, *De corona militis*, c. 3: "Ad omnem progressum atque promotum, ad omnem aditum et exitum, ad vestitum et calciatum, ad lavacra, ad mensas, ad lumina, ad cubilia, ad sedilia, quacumque nos conversatio exercet, frontem signaculo terimus" (Ed. Fr. Œhler, vol. I, p. 423).

[27] Cyprian, *Ad Quirinium Testimonia* (line 248), l. III. For the virtue of the Cross: Origen, *In Jeremiam*, Homily X, n. 2–3 (Baehrens, pp. 72–73), etc.

[28] M. Sulzberger, *loc. cit.*, pp. 371, 413, 447–448.

CHAPTER III

[1] For the historical background to possible influences, suggestions and bibliographical data will be found in La Vallée-Poussin, *L'Inde au temps des Maurya* (1930), pp. 238–243; *Histoire de l'Inde depuis Kaniska* (1935), pp. 297–303. The question is discussed in Jean Filliozat, "Les échanges de l'Inde et de l'Empire romain aux premiers siècles de l'ère chrétienne", in the *Revue historique*, Jan.-Mar. 1949, vol. CCI, pp. 1–29.

[2] For the final example: J. Przyluski, "Bouddhisme et Upanishad", in the *Bulletin de l'Ecole française d'Extrême Orient*, 1933. The same author's numerous memoirs or notes may always be profitably consulted (as, for instance, in the *Mélangs offertes à Franz Cumont*, 1937, vol. II, pp. 925–933, the "Note sur les Trois Hypostases dans l'Inde et à Alexandrie"), always remembering that observations of the utmost subtlety are all too often interspersed with views which are so general that they make criticism well-nigh impossible.

[3] Thus, as regards Asanga, from the penetrating analyses of "The Lotus of the Good Law" by Paul Mus, and the important work by the Abbé E. Lamotte on the *Sandhinirmocanasutra* (Louvain-Paris, 1935, translated from the Tibetan), it appears that this great philosopher of the Mahayana is undoubtedly far more traditional than was thought until recently, so that it is no longer beyond the bounds of

possibility to explain him—in so far as any author may be "explained" by a study of his sources—as entirely a product of India. The *Sandhinirmocanasutra* seems to have been composed in bits and pieces during the second century of the Christian era and fixed in its present state at the beginning of the third (Lamotte, p. 25).

[4] In his work, the *Philosophie de Plotin*, Emile Bréhier devotes a whole chapter to the "Orientalisme de Plotin". The question can be raised with regard to Numenius as well as Basilides.

[5] Clement of Alexandria supplies two brief items of information (*Stromata*, 1, 15 and 3, 7). However little this may be, it is as much as if not more than anything to be found elsewhere.

[6] New additions have been made to this record as a result of the monumental work by Paul Mus—unfortunately still unfinished—*Barabudur, Esquisse d'une histoire du bouddhisme fondée sur la critique archéologique des textes*; Preface by Georges Coedès, Hanoi, Imprimerie d'Extreme Orient, (1935), vols. I and II, 1, pp. 302–802. The same author's study of the "Buddha paré" (*Bulletin de l'Ecole française d'Extrême Orient*, vol. XXVIII, pp. 153–278), in which many of the ideas developed in *Barabudur* are outlined, should also be consulted.

[7] Louis de la Vallée-Poussin, "Note sur les corps du Buddha", in the *Museon* (1913), p. 278. Paul Mus, *Le Buddha paré* (1928), pp. 199–200, and *Barabudur*, vol. II, 1.

[8] English translation in *Sacred Books of the East*, vol. XI, pp. 48–49. The same explanation applies to each of the eight "assemblies". "Digga Nikaya", XVI, 3, 21–23 (P. T. S., II, pp. 109–110). For these texts of the Pali Canon, considered as antecedents of the doctrine of the Trikaya, see O. Stern, "Notes on the Trikaya Doctrine", in *The Commemoration Volume* (Poona, 1937), pp. 389–398. Cf. *Bibliographie bouddhique* (1949), No. 646.

[9] *In Joannem*, vol. I, c. 31 (34) (Preuschen, pp. 38–39).

[10] Vol. II (1929), p. 765, n. 1: "As Christ is a cherub amongst the cherubim": F. Prat, *Origène*, p. liii.

[11] *Origeniana*, l. II, c. 2, q. 3, n. 2–5 (P. G., 17, 797–798). Cf. Prat, *Origène*, p. liv: "Origen rightly says . . . that in the theophanies which were a prelude to His incarnation the Son of God fulfilled the functions of the angels under the name of the Angel of the Lord, or the Angel of the alliance, but he does not say that He assumed their nature in the same way as He took upon Himself our human nature."

[12] "For Christ Himself certainly seems to assume the role of an angel in certain passages of Scripture in which angels speak. Thus, in this last text: 'The angel of the Lord appeared to him in a flame of fire out of the midst of a bush . . . [and] said, I am the God . . . of Abraham, the God of Isaac, and the God of Jacob [Exodus, iii, 2, 6].' Isaias likewise says [i, 6]: 'He shall be called . . . the angel of great counsel.' The Saviour is therefore the 'First' and the 'Last' —not that He is not also the sole intermediary: if He has only been given the names of the two extremes, this is so that it may be quite evident that He has assumed all things unto himself" (Preuschen, p. 39).

[13] *In Genesim*, Homily VIII, n. 8: "Considerandum est quia angelus haec refertur ad Abraham locutus, et quia in consequentibus evidenter hic angelus Dominus ostenditur. Unde puto quod, sicut inter nos homines habitu repertus est ut homo, ita et inter angelos habitu est repertus ut angelus." (Baehrens, 1920, p. 83.)

[14] P. G., 14, 848 A. Compare these passages from Origen with the somewhat different idea which St. Augustine expresses in similar terms, *De Trinitate*, l. III, n. 26: "Ipse tanquam Verbum Dei miro et ineffabili modo erat in angelis, in quorum edictis lex ipsa dabatur" (P. L., 42, 885).

[15] *In cantica canticorum*, Homily II, n. 3.

[16] *In Matthaeum*, vol. XV, n. 24 (P. G., 13, 1324).

[17] Baehrens, p. 285: "Nisi forte hoc intelligi voluit, quod sanguis Jesu non solum in Jerusalem effusus est, ubi erat altare . . . sed et quod supernum altare quod est in celis, ubi et ecclesia primitivorum est, idem ipse sanguis adsperserit; sicut et Apostolus dicit: 'Pacificans per sanguinem crucis suae sive quae in terris sunt, sive quae in celis.' Vis autem scire quia duplex hostia in eo fuit conveniens terrestribus et apta celestibus?"

[18] *The Christian Platonists of Alexandria*, 2nd ed., Oxford (1913), pp. 256–257.

[19] Vol. I, n. 40 (Preuschen, p. 45): cf. vol. XIII, n. 37 (p. 262). See also other passages: *In Leviticum*, Homily II, n. 3, (Baehrens, p. 294); *In Lucam*, Homily X and XLI (Rauer, pp. 71 and 89); *Periarchon* . . .; *In Hebraeos* (Cramer, vol. VII, p. 147); *In Rom.*, 5, 10; *In Matt.*, 13, 8.

[20] G. Bardy, in *Revue biblique*, vol. XXX (1921), p. 122. For the rest, this remark applies equally to the texts quoted above: the idea

to be found in them is analogous to that expressed by St. Irenaeus in *Adversus Haereses*, l. II, 22, 4: "Omnes enim venit per semetipsum salvare: omnes, inquam, qui per eum renascuntur in Deum, infantes, et parvulos, et juvenes, et seniores. Ideo per omnem venit aetatem", etc. (P. G., 7, 784 A).

[21] Cf. H. de Lubac, *Histoire et Esprit, l'intelligence de l'Ecriture d'après Origène*, pp. 289–294.

[22] Cf. Emile Bréhier, *Les idées philosophiques et religieuses de Philon d'Alexandrie* (1908), p. 130. Lagrange, "Vers le Logos de saint Jean", in *Revue biblique*, vol. XXXII (1923), pp. 342–345. J. Lebreton, *Histoire du dogme de la Trinité*, vol. II, p. 663 *et seq.*, etc.

[23] *De somniis*, I, 232–236 (Cohn-Wendland, vol. III, pp. 236–237). Trans. J. Lebreton, *Histoire du dogme de la Trinité*, (1928), vol. II, pp. 670–671. Cf. *Vita Moysis*, I, 66.

[24] Trans. Tisserant, pp. 191–203.

[25] Also known under the names of *Epistula Apostolorum* and, according to an Ethiopian version, *The Testament in Galilee of Our Lord Jesus Christ*. Ed. Carl Schmidt (1919). Cf. G. Bardy, in *Revue biblique* (1921), vol. XXX, pp. 110–134.

[26] Trans. Guerrier, from the Ethiopian (*Patrologia orientalis*, vol. IX, 3, pp. 196–197).

[27] *Loc. cit.*, p. 198.

[28] Cf. *supra*, notes 9 and 12. As a result of a similar kind of imprecision in Judaeo-Christian literature, the heavenly being who was to be manifested in Jesus sometimes seems to have been already incarnate in the ancient prophets (beginning with Adam), sometimes merely to have revealed himself to them.

[29] Ch. VII, trans. Amélineau, p. 7. Text in Carl Schmidt, *Koptischgnostische Schriften* (Leipzig, 1905), vol. I, p. 7. Cf. St. Irenaeus, *Adversus Haereses*, l. II, 24, 6, summarising the doctrine of Basilides: "Et sicut Filium incognitum omnibus (Angelis et Potestatibus) esse, sic et ipsos a nemine oportere cognosci", etc. (P. G., 7, 679 A).

[30] P. G., 7, 702 A.

[31] *Adversus Haereses* l. I, 23, 2: "Hanc Ennoiam exsilientem ex eo . . . degredi ad inferiora et generare angelos et Potestates, a quibus et mundum hunc factum dixit. Posteaquam autem generavit eos, haec detenta est ab ipsis propter invidiam, etc., et omnem contumeliam ab iis pass (a), uti non recurreret sursum ad suum

patrem, usque adeo ut et in corpore humano includeretur, etc."
(P. G., 7, 671 B–C); cf. 3: "et descendisse eum transfiguratum, et
assimilatum Virtutibus, et Potestatibus, et Angelis" (672 B).

[32] *Patrologia orientalis*, vol. XII, Col. 732–733.

[33] C. XIV (P. L., 2, 777–778).

[34] Similarly, the seventh canon of the Council of 553. Cf. G.
Bardy, *Recherches sur l'histoire du texte et des versions latines du 'De
Principiis' d'Origène* (1923), pp. 61–63. It may be remarked, moreover, as Bardy says, that this opinion is not to be found in the *Periarchon*, in Rufinus's translation. It seems hardly right to introduce it
here, as Koetschau does, simply on the strength of these anathemas,
which were directed principally against heretics contemporary
with Justinian; and then to go on to assert that Rufinus has in this
instance abridged and modified Origen's original text.

[35] G. Bareille has clearly shown, *Dict. de théologie catholique*, vol.
IV, Col. 1500, that in Origen's thought such passages do not imply
any Docetism.

[36] *In Matthaeum comm. series*, n. 28 (Klostermann, p. 53). Cf. St.
Irenaeus, *Adversus Haereses*, l. IV, 9, 1; 10, 1 (P. G., 7, 997 A and
1000 A); and, on the Ebionites, St. Epiphanus, *Panarion*, l. I,
vol. II, haer. 30, c. 3 (P. G., 41, 410).

[37] P. G., 14, 1293–1296. Cf. *In Matt. ser.*, n. 92 (Klost., p. 208);
In Lucam, Homily XIV and XVII (Rauer, pp. 97 and 115). On
the other hand, there is a Docetist tendency in Clement, *Stromata*,
VI, 15, 128: "The Saviour, not being κοσμικός, came down
amongst men ὡς κοσμικός" (Staehlin, vol. II, pp. 495–496).
To understand these speculations of Origen's properly, it would
be necessary to analyse his idea of the spiritual creature. Some
suggestions on this point will be found in Jean Daniélou, *Origène*,
p. 212 and especially pp. 243–245, on John the Baptist.

[38] *Adversus Haereses*, l. II, 22, 4 (P. G., 7, 783 C).

[39] Augustine, Sermon CCLXIII, n. 4: "Sic et Dominus manens
Deus, manens Verbum . . . implens angelos, totus ubique, totus in
mundo, totus in Patriarchis, totus in Prophetis, totus in omnibus
sanctis, totus in utero virginis" (P. L., 38, 1215); cf. *Enarratio in
psalmum LXI*, n. 4 (P. L., 730–732). Paulinus of Nola, Letter
XXXVIII, n. 3 (P. L., 61, 359); *Missel de Bobbio, Contestatio domini-
calis* (Lowe, p. 150). Aileran, *Interpretatio mystica progenitorum
Christi*: "Jesum Christum . . . (qui) in patriarchis Patriarcha, in

sacerdotibus Sacerdos, in judicibus judex, in prophetis Propheta, in ducibus Dux, in apostolis Apostolus, in angelis magni consilii Angelus dicitur" (P. L., 80, 329 A).

[40] *Hobogirin*, fasc. 2 (Tokyo 1930), p. 182a.

[41] A parallel analogy may be drawn—between the neo-Platonic doctrine as expressed, for instance, by Proclus, *In Remp. Platonis*, I (Kroll, pp. 91 and 93), concerning the supra-sensible gods that appear to men in the form of angels, and the Mahayanist doctrine of the great Bodhisattvas who are the "words" or the "epiphanies" of the great Buddhas; but this analogy, though perfectly correct, is too general to be really significant. Cf. Origen, *In Joannem*, l. I, 25: "To those who are not able to receive the sun-rays that come from Christ, the saints are there to give light; this light is very inferior, but they are hardly able to receive it, and it is sufficient for them" (Preuschen, p. 31).

[42] The sixth part of Paul Mus's *Barabudur*, which discusses the beginnings of Mahayanist buddhology, throws considerable light on the origin and meaning of this doctrine of the Trikaya.

[43] *De exsecrationibus*, CLXV (Cohn-Wendland, vol. V, p. 304).

[44] *Le messianisme chez les Juifs*, p. 34.

[45] "Le Judaisme avant Jésus-Christ", p. 575. (*Idem* already in Muller.)

[46] "Le Messie chez Philon d'Alexandrie," in *Ephemerides theologicae lovanienses*, Jan. 1935, pp. 29-31. Cf. *infra*, note 69.

[47] *Journal asiatique*, June 1913 (series XI, vol. I), p. 587.

[48] If, for instance, like Huian Tsang, we make a distinction between two kinds of sambhogakaya, it is the parasambhogakaya that is meant here. See the commentary by Paul Mus, *Barabudur*, pp. 776-778.

[49] It is known that the doctrine of the Trikaya is a systematization of a number of elements which are already to be found in symbolic form in the Lotus.

[50] ... Διαφόρους γὰρ ἔχει ὁ Λόγος μορφάς, φαννόμενος ἑκαστω ὡς συμφέρει τῶ βλέποντι, καὶ μηδενί ὑπερ ὅ κωρετ ὁ βλέπων, φανερούμενος. Cf. Clement, *Stromata*, l. VI, 16, 140 (Staehlin, vol. II, p. 503).

[51] Κατὰ τοῦτό γε ἐρεῖς δυνατὸν εἶναι τόν Ἰησοῦν ἔμπροσθεν μὲν τινων μεταμορφωθῆναι ταύτην τὴν μεταμόρφωσῖν ἔμπροσθεν δὲ

ἐτέρων, κατὰ τὸ αὐτὸ καιροῦ μὴ μεταμορφωθῆναι. *In Matthaeum,* vol. XII, n. 36 and 37 (Klostermann, pp. 151–153).

[52] Koetschau, vol. I, pp. 185–186 (or P. G., 11, 896–897). Cf. l. IV, c. 16: "[Those whom He left at the foot of the mountain] were not able to bear the splendour of this glorious and divine transfiguration of the Word. He all but dazzled them, even in the ordinary appearance which He presented to the world. Thus it comes about that those who were unable to look at Him closely enough to discover what was most admirable in Him, could have said: 'There is no beauty in him, nor comeliness: and we have seen him, and there was no sightliness . . . despised and the most abject of men'." (Koetschau, vol. I, pp. 285–286; P. G., 11, 1048 B–C.)

[53] Koetschau, vol. II, pp. 146–149. These are the passages from the *Contra Celsum* which were plagiarised and grossly distorted by Bonaventure des Périers in the famous *Cymbalum Mundi* (1537). Cf. Lucien Febvre *Origène et des Périers, ou l'énigme du* Cymbalum Mundi (1942), p. 88.

[54] *Periarchon,* l. II, c. 1, n. 4 (Koetschau, pp. 109–111); *Contra Celsum,* l. IV, c. 56 (Koetschau, vol. I, p. 329; P. G., 11, 1121); l. III, c. 41 (Koetschau, vol. I, p. 237; P. G., 11, 973 A).

[55] Other passages in Origen of a similar kind: *In Lucam,* Homily III (see *infra,* note 87); *Contra Celsum,* l. VI, c. 68 (Koetschau, vol. II, p. 138; P. G., 11, 1401).

[56] Cf. "The Lotus of the Good Law," ch. I. On the other hand, there is the account given by Huian Tsang, the great Chinese pilgrim to the holy places of Buddhism. In an obscure sanctuary Huian Tsang saw the Buddha sitting on a wall of polished stone, "where only a shadow was to be seen in profile by the eyes of lesser saints, whilst the crowd could see nothing but the naked stone: the chief interest in this is not so much the belief in any change in the object (for in that case when it took place it would have been visible to everybody) as in the importance attached to the classification of men according to the different degrees to which they perceived it". (Paul Mus, *La Lumière sur les six voies,* 1939, p. xiv–xv).

[57] *In Matthaeum,* c. 100 (Klostermann, p. 218). The point is to explain why Judas should have needed to make a sign to point out Jesus to the people who had come to arrest Him. As has been seen already, Origen also takes this example, amongst many others, in the *Contra Celsum.* "Sed etiam unicuique apparebat secundum quod fuerat dignus." He goes on: "Et cum fuisset ipse, quasi non ipse

omnibus videbatur . . . Et non mihi videtur incredibilis esse traditio haec, sive corporaliter propter ipsum Jesum, ut alio et alio modo videretur hominibus, sive propter ipsam Verbi naturam, quod non similiter cunctis apparet."

[58] *In primam Joannis*, I, 1: "Fertur ergo in traditionibus, quoniam Johannes ipsum corpus quod erat extrinsecus tangens, manum suam in profunda misisse, et ei duritiam carnis nullo modo reluctatam esse, sed locum manui praebuisse discipuli. Propter quod etiam inferet, 'et manus nostrae contrectaverunt de verbo vitae'; contrectabilis utique factus est qui venit in carne" (Staehlin, vol. III, p. 210).

[59] "This so-called tradition, which Origen mentions as a 'not incredible' assertion, is accepted without protest by Clement of Alexandria." The *Odes de Salomon* (1911), p. 96. For the "Docetism" of Clement: *ibid.*, p. 94 *et. seq.*, and Tixeront, *Histoire des dogmes*, vol. I (7th ed.), p. 289.

[60] *Excerpta ex Theodoto*, n. 4, 1 and 5, 3 (ed. Casey, in *Texts and Studies*, London, 1934, vol. I, p. 42; ed. F. Sagnard, in *Sources chrétiennes*, XXIII, pp. 58–63).

[61] "It was not even with their bodily eyes that they saw the light. For there is no kinship or affinity between that transcendent light and the fleshly body. But [they saw] to the extent that the Saviour's dynamism and will had granted the flesh the power to contemplate."

[62] Most of these are indicated in the editions of the *Acts of Peter* (Zahn, Vouaux), in chapters XX and XXI, or in the work by J. Flamion, "Les Actes apocryphes de Pierre," *Revue d'histoire ecclésiastique* (1909), pp. 257–258.

[63] Compare St. Irenaeus, *Adversus Haereses*, II, 24, 4 and III, 5, 1 (P. G., 7, 784 and 858). The phrase is in the *Acts of John*, 94, 11, 6. It is also in the *Acts of Peter* (cf. *infra*). See Flamion, *loc. cit.*, p. 249, n. 6. It will be realised that such a phrase can have different meanings according to whether it is applied to the Divinity in general, to the Logos, to Christ in His earthly life, to Christ in His Transfiguration, or to the appearances of Christ to the faithful during the life of the Church.

[64] "And now I shall explain to you what has been read. Our Lord wished me to see His majesty on the holy mountain; but when, with the sons of Zebedee, I saw the splendour of His light, I fell down as one dead, and I closed my eyes, and I heard his voice in a

way that I cannot describe, and I felt as though blinded by His splendour."

[65] *Actes de Pierre*, c. XX and XXI (Vouaux, 1922, pp. 341–343 and 348–355).

[66] For this dependence: Vouaux, pp. 49–53. But, it seems, expressions like "juvenis et senex" are henceforth understood as referring to the opposition between humanity and the Divinity; in the same way, the expression "neque esuriens neque sitiens" seems to be applied to the Divine Nature. As regards the various appearances of Christ, they are no longer inserted as episodes in the life of Jesus, but simply as the result of visions. Cf. Vouaux, pp. 50–51, 69, 71, etc. See also Flamion, *loc. cit.*, pp. 248–251, 257–259, 265–266.

[67] Cf. Photius, *Bibliotheca*, Codex CXIV summarising the work entitled τῶν Ἀποστόλων περίοδοι, by Lucius Charinus, a work which is itself a summary of the *Acts* of Peter, John, Andrew, Thomas and Paul: "Omnia ergo inquinens atque confundens eumdem illum (Christum) et Patrem vocat et Filium, Jactat vero, neque revera hominem factum, sed tantum apparuisse. Varia item forma saepe discipulis visum, nunc juvenem, mox iterum senem, rursumque puerum; nunc majorem, nunc minorem, interdum et maximum, vertice etiam caelum attingentem" (P. G., 103, 390).

[68] St. Irenaeus, *Adversus Haereses*, I, 24, 4 (P. G., 7, 677): "Quapropter neque passum eum, sed Simonem quemdam Cyrenaeum angariatum portasse crucem ejus pro eo: et hunc secundum ignorantiam et errorem crucifixum, transfiguratum ab eo, uti putaretur ipse esse Jesus: et ipsum autem Jesum Simonis accepisse formam, et stantem irrisisse eos. Quoniam enim virtus incorporalis erat, . . . transfiguratum quemadmodum vellet, et sic ascendisse ad eum qui miserat eum, deridentem eos, cum teneri non posset, et invisibilis esset omnibus."

Cf. St. Augustine, *De Trinitate*, l. VIII, c. 4, n. 7: "Nam et ipsius dominicae facies carnis innumerabilium cogitationum diversitate variatur et fingitur, quae tamen una erat, quaecunque erat" (P. L., 42, 951).

[69] *Revue de l'histoire des religions* (1937), vol. CXVI, p. 92.

[70] Judges, vi, 11–18.

[71] Judges, xiii, 1–25. Cf. Adolphe Lods, *Histoire de la littérature hébraïque et juive* (1950), p. 141.

[72] Wisdom xvi, 20–21.

[73] *Epistula CXC*, n. 3 (P. G., 32, 700).

[74] *Loc. cit.*, pp. 218–219.

[75] *In Exodum*, Homily VII, n. 8 (Baehrens, vol. I, pp. 214–217).

[76] Compare also with the passage from the *Sutra des quatre savoirs* (in Huian Tsang, *Siddhi*, ed. la Vallée-Poussin, p. 421): water is a home for fishes, a drink for men, pus and blood for the pretas, space for some contemplatives, etc. It was this idea which gave birth to the theory of the "Nòthing-but-thought" of the Yogacaras.

[77] L. I, c. 6 (Staehlin, vol. I, p. 117).

[78] Cf. Philo, *Allegorical Commentary*, III, 175 (ed. Mangey, vol. I, p. 121): "One can be fed by the Logos in its entirety or by any of its parts . . . The souls of the perfect feed on the Logos in its entirety; let us be content to feed on part of it."

[79] L. IV, c. 18 (Koetschau, vol. I, p. 287). See again *In cantica canticorum comment.*, l. II (Baehrens, p. 171); *In Joannem*, 19, 6 (35–39) (Preuschen, p. 305). The speculations on Scripture are connected with this idea, but the study of these would take us too far from our present purpose. It may be added that they would lead to our discovering new analogies, as well as new contrasts, with Buddhist speculations on the Dharma.

[80] "Lotus", ch. II and XV; cf. in ch. VII, the parable of the Magic Town; and the other canonical text quoted by Paul Demiéville in *Hobogirin*, fasc. 3 (1937), p. 208, art. "Butengo": "The Buddha never lies; his words would remain true even if Mount Sumeru were to move, or the stars to fall, or the palace of the gods to collapse, or the ocean to dry up, or the palaces of the asuras to take the place of the gods' palaces". There is a close connection between this doctrine of the upayas and that of the Trikaya.

[81] Cf. H. de Lubac, "'Tu m'as trompé, Seigneur': le commentaire d'Origène sur Jer., xx. 7" (in *Mémorial Chaine*, 1950, pp. 255–280).

[82] Origen *In Joannem*, l. XIX, n. 6 (Preuschen, p. 305); *In Jeremiam*, Homily XIX, n. 15; Homily XX, n. 1–5 (Klostermann, pp. 173–184), etc.

[83] Cf. Clement, *Stromat.*, l. VII, p. 53 (Staehlin, vol. III, p. 39): "The Gnostic thinks the truth and speaks the truth, except when occasionally, by way of remedy, he acts like a doctor in the

cure of his patients and lies or speaks some untruth, like the Sophists".
An allusion to Plato, *The Republic*, l. III, 377–382. Cf. Origen
himself, *In Joannem*, vol. X, 4 (Preuschen, p. 175).

Cf. St. Gregory the Great, *In evangelia*, l. II, Homily XXIII
(P. L., 76, 1182 C), referring to the disciples at Emmaus: "Nihil
ergo simplex Veritas per duplicitatem fecit, sed talem se eis exhibuit
in corpore, qualis apud illos erat in mente." Or Werner of Saint-
Blaise, "Deflorationes SS. Patrum, sermo de resurrectione" (P.
L., 157, 931 C).

[84] It is a well-known fact that cosmology (in the material and
topographical sense of the word) plays a secondary part, and often
a purely symbolic part, in Christian patristic thought.

[85] *Contra Celsum*, l. VI, c. 77: "Ἔχει δε τι και μυστικὸν ὁ λόγος.

[86] *Ibid.*

[87] Rauer, pp. 20–23. See also Homily I: "Apostoli ipsi viderant
Verbum, non quia adspexerant corpus Domini Salvatoris, sed
quia Verbum viderant" (p. 8).

[88] C. 32 and 35 (Klostermann, pp. 58 and 65). To such an extent
that, in whatever concerns himself, the perfect has already, so to
speak, arrived at the end of time: "Ei ergo qui perfectus est, et ad
consummationem saeculi pervenit quantum ad se, tale apparet
Verbum, ut qui viderit ipsum, dicat: Vidimus gloriam ejus, gloriam
quasi Unici a Patre, plenum gratia et veritate."

[89] L. III (Baehrens, pp. 215–216).

[90] *Contra Celsum*, l. II, c. 63 and 65 (Koetschau, vol. I, p. 280;
or P. G., 11, 896 and 900); *In Matt. ser.*, XXVIII (Klostermann, p.
54); *In Lucam*, Homily IV: οὐδε γὰρ φθαρτοῦ σώματος ὀφθαλμοῖς
ὁμᾶναταὶ τις εδεῖν ἄφθαρτον σῶμα (Rauer, p. 24). Cf. Plotinus,
Enneads, VI, 5, 12: "Often the gods only appear to one man, even
though more than one is there; this is because only one man is
capable of seeing them." Cf. *supra*, n. 53 and 55.

[91] Read on this subject Frédéric Bertrand, S.J., "La Mystique de
Jésus chez Origène" (in *Théologie*, 1951), ch. 1.

[92] As regards this point we have seen the part played by the
Gnostic imagination and Jewish tradition. An indirect echo of
pagan theology can also be perceived. In the "Poimandres", God
is said to be at once hidden and manifest, invisible and visible,
bodiless and yet, πολυσώματος, μᾶλλον δέ παντοσώματος (*Corpus
hermeticum, libellus* V. 10; W. Scott, vol. I, p. 162).

⁹³ P. G., 44, 828. A more literal transcription of the same theme: *Sermon on the Ascension* (P. G., 46, 693 A); the Lord, who contains all things within Himself, puts Himself at the disposal of every individual; and so He does not only become a man amongst men, but also when He comes amongst the angels He lowers Himself to their nature. Cf. St. Maximus the Confessor, *Ambigua* (P. G., 91, 1256 B): "Remaining for ever within Himself, unchanging and unalterable, neither growing nor declining, [God] in His overflowing goodness makes Himself in turn humble towards the humble, great towards the great, and veritable God to those whom He deifies."

⁹⁴ St. Bernard, *In Cantica*, Sermon XXXI, *passim*, n. 7: "Oportet namque pro variis animae desideriis divinae gustum praesentiae variari, et infusum saporem supernae dulcedinis diversa appetentis animi aliter atque aliter oblectare palatum" (P. G., 183, 943 C–D). From the ocean of divinity, said St. John of the Cross, each person draws water with the jug that he takes to it.

⁹⁵ "See the Saviour's look: in Himself always the same, He nevertheless does not always have the same efficacy, but conforms Himself to the merit of each person he reaches: some He inspires with fear, whilst to others He brings rather security and consolation": *In Cantica*, Sermon LVII, n. 2 (P. L., 183, 1050–1051). Cf. William of St. Thierry, *Meditativae orationes*, VIII (Davy, pp. 176–178).

⁹⁶ A possible answer could only be given after a systematic comparison of a considerable number of points; such as for instance, the doctrine of the κατασκευή (Heracleon, in Origen, *In Joannem*, vol. XIII, 44; Preuschen, p. 270) and the Mahayanist doctrine of the gotras; the everlasting "beyond", atita, of the Yogacara mystics and the indefinite typology of the Gnostics of Irenaeus (*Adversus Haereses*, l. IV, 19, 1; P. G., 7, 1030 A–B).

⁹⁷ *Eloge du sambhogakaya*, trans. Chavannes (*Revue de l'histoire des religions*, vol. XXXIV, p. 12). Cf. Paul Mus, *Barabudur*, pp. 657–662. Paul Mus recognises, moreover (p. 38), that the etymology of the word still remains rather dubious, just as the origins of the idea remain obscure.

⁹⁸ Asanga, *Mahayanasutralankara*, IX, 29–30.

⁹⁹ *In Matthaeum*, vol. X, n. 3 (Klostermann, p. 4): ἕν γενόμενοι ἡλιακὸν φῶς . . . καί γένωνται πάντες εἷς ἥλιος.

¹⁰⁰ This is why it seems that Foucher, after comparing the Gospel account of the Transfiguration with Asvaghosa's description

of the *Mahapratiharya*, is very wise to add: "A curious coincidence, but one which, in our opinion, it would be a mistake to attempt to press further." "Le Grand Miracle du Buddha à Cravasti", *Journal asiatique* (Jan.–Feb. 1909), p. 16 (cf. p. 25). For this "great miracle of magic": *idem, La vie du Bouddha d'après les textes et les monuments de l'Inde* (1949), pp. 281–285.

[101] *Acta Joannis*, c. 93, n. 9 (*Acta apostolorum apocrypha*, pars. 2 *a*, vol. I, ed. Bonnet, p. 197).

[102] Wisdom, vii, 3.

[103] P. Mus, *Barabudur*, vol. I, p. 68.

[104] Burnouf, *Le Lotus de la Bonne Loi*, vol. II, p. 576. La Vallée-Poussin, *Bouddhisme, opinions sur l'histoire de la dogmatique*, pp. 233–234.

[105] A similar shade of meaning is brought out by St. Augustine writing of the Spirit of God in his commentary on the beginning of Genesis: "Superferebatur super aquas, non ferebatur ab eis" (*Confessions*, XIII, 4).

[106] Cf. Paul Mus, *Barabudur*, pp. 69–70: "In India from time immemorial the first rule as regards royal etiquette has always been that the monarch must not touch the ground 'for fear of disturbing it'. A palace or a throne, a palanquin, a mount, the skins of animals, carpets or shoes must intercept any contact. The king is a god who appears amongst us but who in reality lives on another level. The Brahmans say more precisely that the reason why he is forbidden by ceremonial to tread upon the earth . . . is because he is the most elevated of creatures. But these are also the very words that Siddharta is made to say in the Pali *Abbhutaccariya* when he takes his first steps forward . . . Nor must we forget that it is a consecration, of the Indian kind. It is a birth . . . The king is born to royalty as a child comes into the world . . . Popular thought was inspired by the most brilliant kind of thing it could see—the ceremonial belonging to its kings; and when, one fine day, the Buddha found himself symbolically set above this world, this was not the result of any abstract speculation about his nature," etc. See again pp. 426–429 and 755: "Buddhists did not have to delve deeply into metaphysics to discover the idea of the Buddha lokottara. The whole tendency was to imagine the Buddha as a king, and it is both the privilege and the servitude of a king not to walk upon the ground . . . The details of the legend leave no doubt that the new conception of a 'supra-mundane' Buddha derived from this." Similarly, Mus, *Le Buddha paré, loc. cit.*

[107] Ch. VI, n. I (trans. Amann, pp. 199–201). Cf. Henri Chirat, "La naissance et les trois premières années de la Vierge Marie dans l'art byzantin", in *Mémorial Joseph Chaine* (Bibliothèque de la Faculté Catholique de Théologie de Lyon, vol. V, 1950), pp. 81–113.

[108] St. Augustine, *De Civitate Dei*, l. IV, c. 11: "Ipsa levet de terra, et vocetur Levana" (P. L., 41, 122). This concerns the one god Jupiter who, according to theorists like Varro, was honoured under the names of many gods and goddesses.

[109] In the *Rig-Veda*, X, 8, 4, and X, 122, 3, Agni, as soon as he is born, travels through the Seven Worlds.

[110] *Majjhima-Nikaya*: "As soon as he was born, the Bodhisattva . . . took seven paces towards the north . . . and roared out like a bull: I am the head of the world!" Cf. the *Nidanakatha*: "He took seven paces in a northerly direction . . . and stopping and standing upright at his seventh pace he said, roaring like a lion: I am at the head of the world!"

[111] For these variants see the long note by the Abbé Etienne Lamotte, in *Le Traité de la Grande Vertu de Sagesse de Nagarjuna*, vol. I (Bibliothèque du Museon, vol. XVIII, Louvain, 1944), pp. 6–10.

[112] Asvaghosa, *Buddhacarita*, First Song. Cf. the *Mahavastu*, II, p. 21: "As soon as he was born he took seven steps forward on the ground, scrutinised the regions of space and uttered the Great Laugh." Other passages in Lamotte, *loc. cit.*

[113] Translation by Lamotte, *loc. cit.*

[114] Paul Mus, *Barabudur*, p. 496; cf. pp. 611–613.

[115] This is also, it seems, the original significance of the "cankrama", the Buddha's covered walk, which was later to find material expression in the architecture of Buddhist monasteries: P. Mus, *op. cit.*, p. 68 and pp. 483–503.

[116] *Mahavastu*, I, p. 159.

[117] René Draguet, "Julien d'Halicarnasse et sa controverse avec Sévère d'Antioche sur l'incorruptibilité du corps du Christ" (Louvain, 1924), pp. 240–248.

[118] A summary of the Buddhology of the *Mahavastu* will be found in A. Barth, *Œuvres*, vol. V, pp. 16–18. Cf. Louis de la Vallée-Poussin, *La Siddhi de Hiuan Tsang*, Appendix, pp. 773–774.

[119] This is also recognised in his own way by Jean Thamar when he writes: "Docetism, according to which the body of Christ is

simply a nirmanakaya, is not heretical in itself but only in its
Western atmosphere of thought in which the body is considered as
an irreducible reality, so that Docetism means denying the humanity
of the Avatara". "Prajnaparamita", in *Etudes asiatiques* (Zürich,
1949), p. 26.

[120] Ananda begged milk to help the Blessed One recover from
an illness. Cf. the invective in the *Vimalakirti*: "Stop, Ananda!
That's enough of such talk! The body of the Tathagata is a Body of
Diamonds . . . Do not slander it! Do not let strangers hear such
crude language." (Quoted by P. Demiéville, art. "Byo" in *Hobogirin*, fasc. 3, 1937, pp. 235-236).

[121] Hippolytus, *Elenchos*, l. VII, c. 38.

[122] Cf. X. le Bachelet, "Hilaire (Saint)", in *Dict. de théologie
catholique*, vol. VI, on the connection between the body of Christ
and His mother: col. 2436-2438; on the passibility of the body of
Christ: col. 2438-2448. Cf. *supra*, note 66.

[123] Cf. *Mahaparinirvanasutra* (T 374-375, 2): "When Sakyamuni
accepted a gift of milk, before he had reached his Awakening, he
still had a human body, which could be fed, could change, and was
subject to human passions and death; but when he received his
disciples' last offering before his Nirvana his Body was made of
Diamonds, an Essence; a permanent Body with no passions, no
birth and no death" (*Hobogirin*, fasc. 2, p. 178 a).

[124] The first of these two theories is in one respect at least similar
to Basilides' theory mentioned earlier; the second theory recalls
that held by Saturninus, Marcion and Mani. One point should also
be noticed in the development of the legend concerning the birth
of Sakyamuni, as described by Alfred Foucher, *La Vie du Bouddha*
(1949), p. 38: "What was originally, and, in the Pali tradition and
the verse rendering of the *Lalitavistara*, remained, a kind of pre-
monitory dream, a presentiment and symbol of the Conception . . .
became in the end, in the prose version of the *Lalitavistara* and the
Mahavastu, a real episode in the life of Sakyamuni; and soon it was
even made into a general law that no Buddha either of the past or
of the future could enter into his mother's womb in any other form
than that of a white elephant."

[125] Nagarjuna, *Mahaprajnaparamitasastra*, I, ch. 1 (trans. Lamotte,
vol. I, p. 20).

[126] As regards the word "ruta" employed by Asanga in the
Mahayanasutralamkara, Sylvain Lévi notes that this word "means in

classical Sanskrit an inarticulate sound, the cry of animals. By its use of this contemptuous word the Mahayana intended to express its scorn of the literal meaning of the Sutras" (p. 6).

[127] Asanga, *op. cit.*, I, 7 (p. 8).

[128] Or, according to another of Asanga's metaphors, *op. cit.*, IX, 34, as the clouds obstruct the sun's rays, so the perversity of creatures obstructs the light that comes from the Buddhas.

[129] An explanation given in a famous stanza of the *Avatamsaka* (T 279) and in the *Vimalakirti* (T 475, 1). In other writings, notably the *Vibhasa* (in which it is stated specifically that this stanza is not canonical: T 1545), it is the linguistic aspect which tends to be emphasised: when the Buddha simply utters one sound, all beings say to themselves: he is speaking my language, it is I he is addressing (Cf. Paul Demiéville, art. "Butsugo"—the Word of the Buddha—and "Button"—the Voice of the Buddha—in *Hobogirin*, fasc. 3, pp. 203a and 215–216).

[130] Ch. xv (trans. Burnouf, p. 198).

[131] The difference between the two truths is made clear in Vasubandhu, *Abhidharmakosa*, c. VI, n. 3–4 (la Vallée-Poussin, pp. 139–141), and in the chief philosophers of the Madhyamika (Nagarjuna, Aryadeva, and later Candrakirti), etc. "The things that are real for ordinary people," says Candrakirti, "are only the truths of error to the wise." *Madhyamikaratara* (trans. la Vallée-Poussin, in *Museon*, vol. XI, 1910, p. 303).

[132] "The Absolute is ineffable, the Absolute transcends all speculation, the Absolute is simple and has the same savour everywhere"; more precisely it is "Non-substantiality, an Emptiness without beginning or end, an Emptiness of inexistence, an Absolute Emptiness, an Unchanging Emptiness". *Samdhinirmocanasutra* (trans. Lamotte, pp. 173, 198, 224–227).

[133] The end of the finger means words and concepts and the phenomena which these signify: all these are apprehended by the vijnana (the consciousness of phenomena, or the discursive intelligence); the direction indicated—indicated, not named—is absolute truth, the object of jnana (knowledge, immediate apprehension), incommunicable. Cf. the *Catuhpratisaranasutra*, Second Refuge, and the *Lankavatarasutra*; passages quoted by E. Lamotte, "La critique d'interprétation dans le Bouddhisme", in *Mélanges Henri Grégoire* (1949), p. 344.

[134] See, for example, Gandeutius of Brescia, *Tractatus II, In Exodum* (Gluck, p. 26). Augustine, *In psalmum CIII*, sermon 4, n. 1 (P. L., 37, 1378). Maximus the Confessor, *Capitula thelogica et œconomica*, centur. II, c. 60–61 (P. G., 90, 1149–1152). Claudius of Turin, *In libros informationum litterae et spiritus super Leviticum* (P. L., 104, 617). Rupert of Deutz, *In Isaiam*, l. II, c. 31 (P. L., 167, 1362); *De Spiritu sancto*, 1. I, c. 6 (P. L., 167, 1475–1476); *In Joannem*, l. VII (P. L., 169, 494–495), etc. For Origen, see my *Histoire et Esprit* (1950), ch. VIII, "Les incorporations du Logos".

[135] Cf. St. Ambrose, *In psalmum LXI*, n. 33 (P. L., 14, 1180). On the other hand, there is an analogy with the Buddha's silence in the remark of the Jewish mystic Eleazar of Worms: "God keeps silent and bears the universe" (quoted by G. G. Scholem, *Les grands courants de la mystique juive*, Fr. trans. 1949, p. 126).

[136] As a general principle one might mention here the principle enunciated by St. Thomas Aquinas, *Summa Theologica*, Part III, q. 3, a. 2: "Hoc quod in Deo est unum et simplex, plurificatur in intellectu nostro, etiamsi immediate a Deo reciperet."

[137] St. Cæsarius of Arles, in his *Expositio in Apocalyps*, has collected a tradition already old in his time: "Gladium vero bis acutum de ore ipsius procedentem, ipsum Christum esse significat, qui et nunc evangelii bona, et prius per Moysen legis notitiam universo orbi protulit, et de quo David similiter ait: Semel locutus est Deus, duo haec audivi (*Opera omnia*, ed. G. Morin, vol. II, p. 212).

[138] Candrakirti, *Madhyamikaratara* (trans. la Vallée-Poussin, in *Museon*, vol. XI, 1910, p. 312).

[139] This is the famous parable of the raft, which was first applied to consciousness and the moral life: *Majjhima-Nikaya*, I, 135 and 261. Louis de la Vallée-Poussin, *Dogme et philosophie du bouddhisme*, p. 93: "The raft is for crossing over the river; when the traveller has reached the other side, he does not take the raft on his shoulders. In the same way, the Dharma . . . is for crossing the waves of passion and error; it destroys all obstacles; but in order to progress further and obtain Beatitude, it is necessary to abandon the Dharma, just as adharma, evil and error, was abandoned in the first place." On the other hand, it is only as the result of misunderstanding that Harnack could write in *Précis de l'histoire des dogmes* (trans. Choisy), pp. 101–102: "Origen thus divests himself of the Christianity of the Church as though it were a veil and throws it away like a crutch."

[140] The Land of the Buddha: "A kind of mystic universe, conceived particularly from the point of view of the connections between the saviour and those whom he is to save"; a Mahayanist notion (P. Demiéville, "Butardo" in *Hobogirin*, fasc. 3, p. 200). As regards the similar Biblical phrase, "to possess the earth", cf. Jacques Guillet, "Thèmes bibliques", coll. *Théologie* (1951), pp. 181–196.

[141] Cf. "The Lotus," ch. XV: "My Land goes on existing, and the beings see it encompassed by fire; it remains in its marvellous condition and they see it full of a hundred different kinds of miseries."

[142] As is well known, the Buddhist ideal is a perfectly uniform, flat landscape. The Land of Buddha "has for its level ground pure morality" (*Hobogirin, loc. cit.*, p. 201a). Cf. Isaiah xl., 3–4; Baruch, v. 7. The Biblical idea is, however, quite different, and Isaiah xxxiv, 11 supplies a perfect contrast: "A line shall be stretched out upon it to bring it to nothing, and a plummet unto desolation."

[143] *Vimalakirti nirdesa sutra* (*Hokei Izumi*, pp. 64–65); quoted by Paul Mus, *Barabudur*, pp. 614–615. Cf. Paul Demiéville, "Butardo" (*Hobogirin*, fasc. 3, p. 201b): "From the Buddha's point of view the lands are always pure; it is in the eyes of inferior beings that there are impure ones; in reality they are all the same."

[144] A similar story will also be found in the Jewish mystical tradition of the Hekaloths, interpreting an anecdote found in the Talmud. One who was unworthy entered paradise, a magnificent royal residence made entirely of brilliant marble: "The angels who were at the gates troubled his senses. . . . Driven forward by them, he found himself hurled into a boiling river of lava. . . . At the gate of the sixth residence appeared thousands, millions of waves of water which hurled themselves against him; but there was not a drop of water, but only the ethereal brightness of the marble slabs, etc." G. G. Scholem, *Les grands courants de la mystique juive*, Fr. trans. (1950), pp. 66 and 376.

[145] "Entretiens sur la doctrine du Saint-Esprit." Quoted by W. Lossky, *Essai sur la théologie mystique de l'Eglise d'Orient* (1944), p. 226, and by E. Behr-Sigel, "Prière et sainteté dans l'Eglise russe" (coll. *Russie et Chrétienté*, 1950), p. 119.

[146] Cf. E. Behr-Sigel, *op. cit.*, p. 74: "In Russian hagiography the saint is a man who has received the Holy Spirit, and who, as a result of this gift, sees what is always there but is not seen by others,

the interaction of heavenly and earthly realities; a man who is veritably visited by messengers from heaven and who is sometimes able to assist others in sharing his supernatural vision."

[147] *Op. cit.*, p. 221. Cf. Palamas, *Homily on the Transfiguration*: "The light of Our Lord's Transfiguration never either began or ended, it remained uncircumscribed and imperceptible by the senses even though it was seen by bodily eyes . . . but by a transmutation of their senses Our Lord's disciples passed from the flesh to the Spirit."

[148] Nor the following assertion by Nicolas Berdyaev, when he says that his thought is "directed particularly towards a revolution consciousness" and that in his opinion "truth is the victory over objectification, i.e. over illusion, the illusory character of objective being". For he nevertheless goes on to state: "If the world is fallen, the fault does not lie with our consciousness of the world, as L. Chestov maintained for instance, but in the depths of the existence of the world." *Essai de métaphysique eschatologique*, pp. 7, 55, 81.

[149] *Ambiguorum liber* (P. G., 91, 1309 B) . . . ὡς κατ' αὐτὸν λοιπὸν μή ἐχούσης πρὸς τὸν παράδεισον διαφορὰν τῆς καθ᾿ἡμᾶς οἰκουμένης . . .

[150] St. Ambrose, *Epist. XLVI, ad Ambrosium Sabinum* (P. L., 16, 1146–1148).

[151] Cf. St. Leo the Great, *Sermo XXI*, c. 2 (P. L., 51, 192).

[152] The whole letter is aimed at Apollinaris, "qui non potest audire quod Dominus noster Jesus pro nobis servitutem susceperit in istius corporis susceptione. . . . Hoc munimentum, haec sepes est fidei nostrae; qui hanc destruit, destretur ipse . . ." (n. 1, col. 1145 C). "Quaero quid sit, 'formam servi accipiens'? Sive dubio perfectionem naturae et conditionis humanae" (n. 7, col. 1147 C). "Nec advertunt quod haec Christi gloria sit, quia servitutem suscepit in corpore suo, ut libertatem omnibus redderet; peccata nostra portavit, ut mundi peccatum tolleret" (n. 12, col. 1149 C), etc.

[153] If the idea mentioned by Lossky were to be ever so slightly generalised, the result would be, as Mgr. Charles Journet very truly says, "that, Christ having always been in glory, His suffering would only be apparent".

[154] E. Behr-Sigel, *op. cit.*, p. 120. For Dostoievsky, cf. my *Drama of Atheist Humanism* (English edition published by Sheed and Ward, 1949), Part III, ch. III, section 3, "The New Birth".

[155] Newman, "Christ Hidden in the World", in *Parochial and Plain Sermons*, IV (1909), p. 246.

[156] Simone Weil, *Waiting on God* (1951), pp. 113–114.

[157] Deuteronomy, iv, 24.

[158] Fr. Louis Bouyer, *Vie de Saint Antoine par Saint Athanase* (1950), p. 196 (commenting on St. Paul).

[159] *In Matthaeum*, XVII, 19 (Klostermann, pp. 639–640); *In Numeros*, Homily XIII, n. 1–2 (Baehrens, p. 109); *In Psalmum LXXIV*, 4 (P. G., 12, 1533 D), etc. Cf. *Histoire et Esprit*, pp. 235–236. Similarly for the appearance of Christ on the Day of Judgment. Cf. St. Gregory the Great, *In Ezechielem*, l. I, Homily VII, n. 20, commenting on the *"crystallum horribile"* of Ezechiel i. 22: "Et mirum quomodo in hoc crystallo conveniat pulchritudo cum pavore. Sed omnibus vera scientibus constat quia Redemptor humani generis cum judex apparuerit, et speciosus justis, et terribilis erit injustis. Quem enim mansuetum aspiciunt electi, hunc eumdem pavendum atque terribilem conspiciunt reprobi" (P. L., 76, 850 A).

[160] See, for example, St. Bonaventure, *In II Sent.*, d. 33, a. 3, q. 1, ad 5m: "Sicut idem ignis magis cruciat majorem peccatorem quam minorem, sic in eodem igne patiuntur corpora eorum qui peccaverunt peccato actuali. Parvulorum vero corpora, etiamsi in ipsis ignibus infernalibus volutentur, passionem non sentiunt,—et tamen non habent impassibilitatis dotem . . ."

[161] Consider, by way of example, the central theme of the *Bhadramayaravyakarana*; the magician Bhadra, aiming to compromise Sakyamuni, invited him and his disciples to a feast which he created by magic on a heap of dirt. The Buddha in his omniscience foresaw that it was a trap; nevertheless he accepted the invitation and used his power to prevent Bhadra from making the imaginary feast disappear; then he preached on the subject of maya and Bhadra was converted. (Cf. *Bibliographie bouddhique*, 1949, n. 82, from the edition of the Tibetan text by K. Régamey, Warsaw, 1938). Cf. Paul Masson-Oursel, *La philosophie en Orient* (1938), p. 106: "India never separates the idea from the act, and thoughts for her are a kind of magic." The importance which Buddhism attaches to "the marvel of psychic powers" is well known. (Cf. *Anguttara Nikaya*, I, 70; *Samuyutta Nikaya*, V, 282, etc.). It is also a well-known fact that the highest mysticism is often near to magic—which it interiorises without rejecting it—when there is an absence of prayer or faith in a personal God.

[162] Quoted by Nagarjuna, *Mahaprajnaparamitasastra*, I, ch. 1 (trans. Lamotte, p. 3). Cf. Vasubandhu, *Vimsakita*, n. 4–8 (trans. Sylvain Lévi, pp. 46–49); or Santideva, *Bodhicaryavatara*, c. IV, v. 47 (trans. L. Finot, p. 51).

[163] Ch. XV (trans. Burnouf, p. 192).

[164] Cf. Burnouf, *Introduction à l'étude du bouddhisme indien*, p. 478.

[165] Asanga, *op. cit.*, VI, 5 (trans. Sylvain Lévi, p. 52).

[166] I have given my own opinions on this matter in my essay, "Nietzsche mystique" (*Affrontements mystiques*, 1950).

[167] Paul Demiéville, "Sur l'authenticité du Ta Tch'eng k'i sin louen (*Mahayanasraddhotpaddasastra*)", in *Bulletin de la Maison franco-japonaise*, (1929), vol. II, p. 71.

[168] *Mahayanasutralamkara*, c. VI (trans. Sylvain Lévi, p. 51).

[169] Cf. *supra*, "Two Cosmic Trees". Paul Claudel should be consulted again—"Un poète regarde la croix," p. 240: "These two all-powerful arms above us which have just taken wing—'Arise', they say, 'and come! . . .' The God whom we adore is not only erect, He is lifted up, He is stretched to the extremest limit, there is not a fibre of His Body in which power is not active! He is above all, He is dependent on nothing, but it is we who are dependent on Him and we who hold on to Him, indissolubly! He is there for ever between heaven and earth, hanging as our intermediary. He is a God in fullest activity. He is not only raised up, but His eyes are fixed on His Father, He is absolutely absorbed in the effort to raise everything, including us, up to Him." And p. 65: "During those three hours of agony and labour on the Cross, all sorts of bonds are made and resolved and lead on to others; a new world is created athwart the other, to the sound of the Seven Words that come down from the Cross." See *supra*, ch. II. note 112.

NOTE TO THE ENGLISH EDITION

The following works mentioned in the text have appeared in English editions:

BUDDHIST WRITINGS

Anguttara Nikaya	Edited R. Morris and E. Hardy (Pali Text Society, 1885–1900). Trans. as *Gradual Sayings* by F. L. Woodward and E. M. Hare (Pali Text Society, 1932–6)
Bodhicaryavatara	Trans. (abridged) by L. D. Barnett (*Wisdom of the East Series*, London, 1909)
Dhammapada	Trans. F. Max Müller (*Sacred Books of the East*, 1881)
Dipavamsa	Trans. H. Oldenberg, 1879
Digga Nikaya	Trans. Rhys Davids (*Sacred Books of the Buddhists*, 2 vols., 1899–1921)
Itivuttaka	Trans. J. H. Moore (Columbia Press, New York, 1906)
Jatakamala	*Sacred Books of the Buddhists*, 1895
Lankavatarasutra	Trans. D. T. Suzuki (George Routledge, 1932)
Majjhima-Nikaya	Trans. Lord Chalmers (*Sacred Books of the Buddhists*, 2 vols., 1926–7)
Mahavamsa	Trans. W. Geiger and M. H. Bodl, 1912
Mahavastu	Vols. I and II trans. J. J. Jones (*Sacred Books of the Buddhists*, Nos. 16, 18). Vol. III is in preparation
Nidanakatha	In *Buddhist Birth Stories*, T. W. Rhys Davids, 1880
Prajnaparamita Hridaya Sutra	*Sacred Books of the East*, vol. XLIX, 1894
Samyutta Nikaya	Ed. L. Feer (Pali Text Society, 5 vols., 1884–98. Trans. as *Kindred Sayings* by Mrs. Rhys Davids and F. L. Woodward

	(Pali Text Society Translation Series, 5 vols., 1917–30)
Siksasamuccaya	Pub. John Murray, 1922
Sutta-Nipata	Trans. Sir M. Coomaraswami, 1874
Theragatha (Psalms of the Brethren)	Trans. Mrs. Rhys Davids (Pali Text Society Translation Series, 1913)
Vinaya Pitaka	Trans. T. W. Rhys Davids and H. Oldenberg (*Sacred Books of the East*, 3 vols.)

HINDU WRITINGS

Atharva-Veda *Rig-Veda*	Ed. Max Müller
Chandogya Upanishad, *Katha Upanishad,* *Svastasvatara Upanishad,* *Taittvya Upanishad*	In *Sacred Books of the East*, vols. I and XV, trans. Max Müller

English readers may also be interested in two books on Buddhism —*Buddhism* by Christmas Humphreys (Penguin Books, 1951) and *Living Thoughts of Gotama the Buddha* (*Living Thoughts Library*, Cassell, 1948). This is referred to in the text as *La Pensée de Gotama le Bouddha* by A. K. Coomaraswamy and I. B. Horner.

GLOSSARY OF NAMES AND TERMS

Abhidharmakosa: see Vasubandhu.

Ajanta: A famous site in Central India; underground temples with Buddhist frescoes.

Amaravati: Another famous archaeological site of Buddhist India.

Amida, Amidism: see Amitabha.

Amitabha or Amitayus (Jap.: Amida): One of the transcendent Buddhas conceived by the Mahayana. Probably of Persian origin. The cult of Amitabha developed and gave rise to Amidism, which is now to be found all over the Far East.

Ananda: The Buddha's favourite disciple, who has been compared with St. John the Apostle. Full of kindness and human feeling. It was he who cared for Sakyamuni and to him the Master addressed his final instructions. He was subsequently harshly treated by the strictly monastic tradition.

Andhra: A kingdom of Southern India which during the first centuries A.D. seems for a long time to have been hostile to Buddhism.

Arhat: see Hinayana.

Aryadeva: A philosopher of the Madhyamika School, Nagarjuna's chief disciple, third century. The author of *Satasastra*.

Asanga: The leading philosopher of the Vijnanavadin or Yogacara School, the most important school of the Great Vehicle, which taught the idealist doctrine of "Nothing-but-thought" (Vijnana-matra), the "thought-receptacle" or "thought-that-contains-everything" (Alayavijnana). He came from Peshawar in the Gandhara and lived during the Gupta dynasty in the fifth century A.D. The author of the *Mahayanasutralamkara* and other important works.

Asoka: Emperor of the vast Maurya Empire (whose capital was at Pataliputra). He came to the throne c. 273 B.C. After his conversion to Buddhism he displayed tremendous zeal for the moral welfare of his subjects and the spread of the Buddhist faith, as is shown by his famous "Edicts", which are inscribed on stone. Legend attributes to him the summoning of a great council at Pataliputra in 247 B.C. The most powerful protector that Buddhism has ever had.

Asokavadana: The Asoka legends: an important series of miraculous stories (which have been studied by Jean Przyluski).

Ashvaghosha: A brilliant Buddhist writer, described by Sylvain Lévi as "the St. Augustine of the Sanskrit Canon". According to tradition he lived in North-West India near King Kanishka (first century A.D.). Amongst the main works attributed to him are: *Buddhacarita* (a poem on the life of the Buddha) and *Sutralamkara* (a literary and hagiographical illustration of the sutras).

Atharva-Veda: see *Veda*.

Avalokitesvara or Avalokita: A great Bodhisattva corresponding to the Buddha Amitabha as his Word or appearance. The object of a widespread cult in Tibet and the whole of the Far East. Cf. the recent book by Mlle. M. T. de Mallmann:" Introduction a l'étude d'Avalokitesvara" (*Annales du Musée Guimet*, 1948). (Ch. Koang-chu-yinn; Jap. Kwannon).

Avici: The Buddhist universe is made up of three parts, of which the lowest is Kamadhatu (the world of desire), and this includes, besides our earth, a whole series of paradises (svargas) and hells, temporary places of pleasure or pain. Avici is the most terrible of these hells, and suffering there is incessant.

Avidya: Ignorance; the first (or last) of the twelve links forming the chain of the Pratityasamutpada (the law of the Twelve Nidanas, or conditions). It lies at the root of desire, which itself lies at the root of suffering.

Bharhut: An important archaeological site rich in Buddhist sculpture (Central India).

Bhikshu: A monk (fem. Bhikshuni).

Bodhi: Enlightenment, Awakening, through which one becomes a Buddha.

Bodhisattva: see Hinayana-Mahayana.

Buddha, Dharma, Sangha: The "Three Jewels" (triratna) that contain the whole of Buddhism: the Buddha, the Law, the Community. All converts to Buddhism recite a formula which is known as the "Triple Refuge", as, for instance: "I take my refuge in the Buddha, the best of men, in Dharma, the best of detachments, in Sangha, the best of brotherhoods".

Buddhahood: The condition reached through Enlightenment (Bodhi), ineffable, as what is revealed is ineffable. The final intuition at the moment when "all obstacles disappear" (Asanga);

the condition in which all Buddhas share—and all beings are called upon to become Buddhas. "As space is to be found everywhere throughout all the multitudinous variety of forms, so Buddhahood is to be found everywhere throughout the multitudinous variety of beings" (Asanga).

Candrakirti: A philosopher of the Madhyamika School, end of sixth or beginning of seventh century A.D. His *Madhyamakavatara* is a commentary on the *Madhyamikasastra* by Nagarjuna.

Devadatta: Sakyamuni's cousin, who out of hatred never stopped persecuting him and laying snares for him. The Master triumphed over him by magic and by his gentleness.

Dhammapada: A small book of the Pali Canon, "the most beautiful and most comprehensive collection of verse" (Solange Bernard).

Dharma: A highly complex Indian notion; same root as the Latin *firmus*; anything on which one can build. Solid learning or religious truth; law, moral code (and also morality). The Buddhist Dharma is the law of salvation. In the Mahayana the word takes on a wider meaning. See Trikaya.

Dharmakaya: see Trikaya.

Gandhara: A province in north-west India, to which Buddhism spread at about the beginning of the Christian era. The cradle of Græco-Buddhist art.

Gridhrakuta: A mythical mountain on whose summit Sakyamuni is said to have taught the doctrines of the Great Vehicle when the mere "hearers", the initiates of the Little Vehicle, had departed.

Hinayana and Mahayana (The Little and Great Vehicles): The two great divisions of Buddhism (which took place without any real schism) at the beginning of the Christian era. "Little Vehicle" was a nickname given it by its rival branch, the initiates of the "Great Vehicle".

The Hinayana ideal is the Arhat, the monk who seeks his own deliverance, the "saint for his own sake". The Mahayana ideal is the Bodhisattva, who tries to help others and assist them along the way of salvation.

The Mahayana attaches less importance to purely monastic practices; it cultivates the worship of the Buddha, or rather Buddhas, of which it recognises an infinite number; it adds a number of other sacred books to the Hinayana Canon.

Huian Tsang: The most famous of the great Chinese pilgrims who went to India to venerate the holy places (he was there from 630 to 644) and bring back the sacred books. A great man of religion, a great philosopher, a great translator; author of the *Vijnap-timatrata siddhi* (i.e. an exposition of the doctrine of "Nothing-but-idea"). He described his travels in his Memoirs, which were translated by Stanislas Julien and recently published with a commentary by René Grousset.

Itivuttaka: "The Traditions". One of the fifteen books of the *Khuddaka Nikaya* (a collection of short stories), which is itself one of the five books of the Sutta Pitaka (see Tripitaka).

Jataka: "The Births." An account of the Buddha's earlier lives, both as an animal and as a human. An immense collection of tales, many of which date from pre-Buddhist times. In the Canon it is part of the *Khuddaka Nikaya* (see Tripitaka). "These evocative tales, written in a richly human style, bring to life simple scenes that can be highly moving and are always highly edifying" (Solange Bernard).

Jina: A conqueror. Like "Buddha" (the "Awakened One"), a common name. This name was given to the founder of Jainism, an Indian religion more or less contemporary with Buddhism, but the Buddhas are also said to be Jinas.

Kalpa: A period of cosmic time.

Kassapa: An ascetic who was converted by the Buddha; the typical Arhat; immediately on the Buddha's entry into nirvana (i.e. on his death) he summoned the "First Council" at Rajagriha.

Kumarajiva: One of the chief translators of Buddhist books into Chinese. He arrived in China in 402. Fifty important works have his signature; and he is said to have had more than three thousand pupils. His dissolute behaviour does not seem to have had any adverse effect on the success of his teaching.

Lalitavistara: "The Development of the Games." A composite work; a fabulous biography of the Buddha, who comes down like a god "to play in the world of human beings". It is supposed to be Sakyamuni's own account of his life.

Lokottaravadin: A sect who believe that everything concerning the Buddha is "lokottara" (supernatural).

Mahavagga: "The Great Collection": a canonical work, part of the *Vinaya Pisaka*. See *Tripitaka.*

Mahaparinibbanasutta: An account of the Buddha's last days and death (and entry into perfect nirvana). Part of the *Digha Nikaya* (a collection of long sutras) in the *Sutta Pitaka*. See Tripitaka.

Mahavastu: "The Great Questions." Contains some very old parts (in both prose and verse), relating the main events in the Buddha's life. In the Great Vehicle it is considered to be a canonical work, although it is not part of the "nine Dharmas" that were later added to the "Three Baskets".

Majjhima-Nikaya: "The collection of Medium Pieces." One of the five parts of the *Sutta Pitaka*. (These five parts are—long, medium, collected, additional, short.)

Mathura: The "City of the Gods", the first main stage in Buddhist expansion towards the West.

Milarepa: A Tibetan mystical poet of the eleventh century; a disciple of Marpa. In his poems the ideal of universal detachment appears in a peculiar light, in which the spirit of the Great Vehicle is mingled with the solitary aspirations of the wildest kind of anchorite.

Nagarjuna: The leading figure in the Madhyamika School of the Great Vehicle; end of the second century A.D. He has been said to be "the outstanding Buddhist teacher after the Buddha himself" (Söderblom).

Nirvana (Pali: Nibbana): The final state of one who has obtained deliverance. He has escaped from samsara (the wheel of rebirth). There are differing conceptions of nirvana.

Parinirvana: Complete or perfect nirvana, the "nirvana without residue", reached at the end of the existence in which Enlightenment has been gained.

Prajnaparamita: "The Perfection of Wisdom", "Transcendent Wisdom". One of the "nine Dharmas" (nine sacred works) proper to the Mahayana. A collection eight thousand verses long teaching the doctrine of the Void: "The Buddha himself, O respectable Subhuti, is like an illusion". About the beginning of the Christian era.

Pratyekabuddha: A Buddha for his own sake, inferior to the great Buddhas who announce the law of deliverance to creatures.

Rig-Veda: see *Veda*.

Saddharmapundarika: "The Lotus of the Good Law": the third of the "nine Dharmas" (books of the Law); a work which is fundamental to the Mahayana (translated by Burnouf, 1852). Esoteric teaching put into the mouth of Sakyamuni preaching before myriads of bodhisattvas after the mere "hearers" (i.e. the initiates of the Hinayana) had departed.

Sakyamuni: The chief name given to the founder of Buddhism (the sage or monk of the Sakyas—i.e. of the clan of the Sakyas in Northern India on the frontier of Nepal), sixth to fifth century

B.C. It was his "Enlightenment", his "Awakening" (Bodhi), which made him a Buddha, the Buddha of our world.

Sambhoga: The communal life of the sangha (living and learning together); the communal joy shared by the Bodhisattvas in the "Land of Buddha", sometimes called the "Land of Sambhoga".

Santideva: c. 650–700. Madhyamika School. His *Bodhicarya-vatara* (an introduction to the practice of Bodhi) is a treatise on the spiritual life according to Mahayanist principles; it has been compared to our *Imitation*.

Sariputra (Pali: Sariputta): A young monk who, with his friend Maudalyayana (Pali: Moggalana), was converted by Sakyamuni shortly after the Sermon of Benares. They were attracted by the ideal of a pure, serene life as manifested in the Buddha.

Sujata: A peasant woman who gave Sakyamuni a bowl of milk shortly before the night of Bodhi.

Sutta Nipata: "A collection of instructions in which there is a great deal more feeling and poetry than in the other collections" (Solange Bernard).

Tathata: According to the Yogacara School, absolute Nature, but not distinct from thought; absolute reality, but identical with the Void. It is nirvikalpa, "without ideas", i.e. beyond discursive knowledge.

Tathagata: A name which the Buddha gives himself in the Pali Scriptures, a common name like "Buddha". The most probable meaning is, "He who has arrived, who has reached his aim". Or it may mean, "He who comes like his predecessors".

Theragatha: "Verses of the Elders". Short life-histories of monks. Forms part of the *Khuddaka Nikaya* (the short collection).

Trikaya: One of the main doctrines of the Mahayana, of which a classical exposition is to be found in Asanga. He distinguishes the "Three Bodies" (Trikaya) of the Buddha: Dharmakaya (the body of the law, the essential body), which is the same for all Buddhas; Sambhogakaya (the body of beatitude or communion), a manifestation of the Dharmakaya to the Bodhisattvas; Nirmanakaya (the body subject to change), the sensible appearance to creatures of becoming—the Buddhas as they have appeared and will appear on earth. Dharmakaya is identical in essence with the Scriptures, indeed with the essence of all reality (which is essentially a "void"). Cf. Paul Masson-Oursel, *La philosophie en Orient*, p. 107: "A Buddha does not simply incarnate the Law (as a 'body of the Law', Dharmakaya); he makes himself available to all and creates a common feeling of sympathy (as a 'body of collective joy', Sambhogakaya); he is an artist in prestige (as Nirmanakaya)."

Tripitaka (Pali: Tipitaka): "The Three Baskets". The Canon of the Scriptures, in imitation of the "Three Vedas" of the Brahmans, collected according to this saying made on the death of Sakyamuni: "The Law of the Omniscient One was like a scattering of divine flowers; Ananda went and gathered them up into three separate baskets." The Buddha preached in the Magadha dialect, but the two main languages in which the Scriptures were originally written were Sanskrit and Pali.

The Canon (Pali) has three parts: the *Vinava Pitaka*, which is concerned with monastic discipline; the *Sutta Pitaka*, which is a collection in five books of the Buddha's sermons and edifying stories; and the *Abhidhamma Pitaka*, a collection of philosophical and didactic works.

The whole forms an immense body of writing accumulated over several centuries. The Mahayana adds still more books.

Upanishad: The *Vedas* have commentaries known as Brahmanas; each Brahmana has a special section or a chapter of theology which is designed to be meditated in the forest (aranya). The *Upanishad* is one part of this section. The word has assumed the meaning of a "confidential doctrine". The oldest Upanishads date from about the seventh century B.C.

Upasaka: Buddhist lay disciples who have not fully entered upon the Way of Enlightenment.

Vasubandhu: Asanga's brother, converted by him to the Mahayana. Is this the Vasubandhu who wrote the *Abhidharmakosa*, the *Summa* of the Little Vehicle?

Veda: Veda = knowledge, from "vid" = to know.

The *Vedas* are four big collections of sacred hymns, the oldest literary works in existence in India.

Rig-Veda: "The Veda of Verses", the oldest (1,028 hymns).

Yagur-Veda: "The Veda of Sacrificial Formulas".

Sama-Veda: "The Veda of Melodies".

Atharva-Veda: "The Veda of Charms", very different from the other three; 731 hymns, very much like magical incantations.

Yogacara: A mystical idealist school of the Mahayana, another name for the Vijnanavadin. See Asanga.